DoD Information Security Program: Overview, Classification, and Declassification

DODM 5200.01, Volume 1, February 24,

2012 Incorporating Change 3 Jan 17, 2025

DoD Information Security Program: Overview, Classification, and Declassification

DODM 5200.01, Volume 1, February 24, 2012

Incorporating Change 3 Jan 17, 2025

NISPOM CENTRAL

RED BIKE PUBLISHING, LLC

DoD Information Security Program: Overview, Classification, and Declassification

Printed by: Red Bike Publishing

www.nispomcentral.com

Red Bike Publishing publishes books in print and electronic format. Some publications appearing in print may not be available in electronic book format. Red Bike Publishing also publishes books in electronic format. Some publications appearing in print may not be available in electronic book format.

ISBN: 978-1-936800-38-4

About Red Bike Publishing...

Mission:

NISPOM Central was created to provide NISPOM books, training and resources all in one location. NISPOM Central is part of Red Bike Publishing: Our company is registered as a government contractor company with the CCR and VetBiz (DUNS 826859691). Specifically, we are a service disabled veteran owned small business.

Vision:

Red Bike Publishing will be valued for its one-of-a-kind niche publishing and ability to positively impact our customers.

If you want more information about NISPOM compliance check out our video and training.

https://www.nispomcentral.com

Department of Defense
MANUAL

NUMBER 5200.01, Volume 1
February 24, 2012
Incorporating Change 3, Effective January 17, 2025

USD(I&S)

SUBJECT: DoD Information Security Program: Overview, Classification, and Declassification

References: See Enclosure 1

1. PURPOSE

a. Manual. This Manual is composed of several volumes, each containing its own purpose. The purpose of the overall Manual, as authorized by DoD Directive (DoDD) 5143.01 (Reference (a)) and DoD Instruction (DoDI) 5200.01 (Reference (b)), is to reissue DoD 5200.1-R (Reference (c)) as a DoD manual (DoDM) to implement policy, assign responsibilities, and provide procedures for the designation, marking, protection, and dissemination of controlled unclassified information (CUI) and classified information, including information categorized as collateral, sensitive compartmented information (SCI), and Special Access Program (SAP). This guidance is developed in accordance with Reference (b), Executive Order (E.O.) 13526 and E.O. 13556, and parts 2001 and 2002 of title 32, Code of Federal Regulations (References (d), (e), and (f)). This combined guidance is known as the DoD Information Security Program.

b. Volume. This Volume:

(1) Describes the DoD Information Security Program.

(2) Provides guidance for classification and declassification of DoD information that requires protection in the interest of the national security.

(3) Cancels Reference (c) and DoD O-5200.1-I (Reference (g)).

(4) Incorporates and cancels Directive-Type Memorandums 04-010 (Reference (h)) and 11-004 (Reference (i)).

2. APPLICABILITY. This Volume:

a. Applies to OSD, the Military Departments, the Office of the Chairman of the Joint Chiefs of Staff and the Joint Staff, the Combatant Commands, the Office of the Inspector General of the Department of Defense, the Defense Agencies, the DoD Field Activities, and all other organizational entities within the Department of Defense (hereinafter referred to collectively as the "DoD Components").

b. Does NOT alter existing authorities and responsibilities of the Director of National Intelligence (DNI) or of the heads of elements of the Intelligence Community pursuant to policies issued by the DNI. Consistent with Reference (b), SCI shall be safeguarded in accordance with the policies and procedures issued by the DNI, as implemented by Volumes 1 - 3 of DoDM 5105.21 (Reference (j)) and other applicable guidance.

3. DEFINITIONS. See Glossary.

4. POLICY. It is DoD policy, in accordance with Reference (b), to:

a. Identify and protect national security information and CUI in accordance with national level policy issuances.

b. Promote information sharing, facilitate judicious use of resources, and simplify management through implementation of uniform and standardized processes.

c. Classify and declassify national security information as required by References (d) and (f).

5. RESPONSIBILITIES. See Enclosure 2.

6. PROCEDURES. See Enclosures 3 through 5.

7. INFORMATION COLLECTION REQUIREMENTS.

The Annual Report on Classified Information referenced in paragraph 7.m. of Enclosure 2 of this Volume has been assigned Report Control Symbol (RCS) DD-INT(AR)1418 in accordance with the procedures in Volume 1 of DoDM 8910.01 (Reference (k)).

8. RELEASABILITY. **Cleared for public release**. This Volume is available on the DoD Issuances Website at https://www.esd.whs.mil/DD.

9. SUMMARY OF CHANGE 3. The change to this volume removes language regarding original classification authority (OCA) and security classification guides in accordance with Paragraph 1.2. of DoD Manual 5200.45 (Reference (bm)).

10. EFFECTIVE DATE. This Volume is effective February 24, 2012.

Michael G. Vickers
Under Secretary of Defense
for Intelligence

Enclosures
1. References
2. Responsibilities
3. DoD Information Security Program Overview
4. Classifying Information
5. Declassification and Changes in Classification
6. Security Classification Guides
Glossary

TABLE OF CONTENTS

ENCLOSURE 1

REFERENCES

(a) DoD Directive 5143.01, "Under Secretary of Defense for Intelligence and Security (USD(I&S))," October 24, 2014, as amended
(b) DoD Instruction 5200.01, "DoD Information Security Program and Protection of Sensitive Compartmented Information (SCI)," April 21, 2016
(c) DoD 5200.1-R, "Information Security Program," January 14, 1997 (hereby cancelled)
(d) Executive Order 13526, "Classified National Security Information," December 29, 2009
(e) Executive Order 13556, "Controlled Unclassified Information," November 4, 2010
(f) Parts 2001 and 2002 of title 32, Code of Federal Regulations
(g) DoD O-5200.1-I, "Index of Security Classification Guides (U)," September 1, 1996 (hereby cancelled)
(h) Directive-Type Memorandum 04-010, "Interim Information Security Guidance," April 16, 2004 (hereby cancelled)
(i) Directive-Type Memorandum 11-004, "Immediate Implementation Provisions of Executive Order 13526, "Classified National Security Information," April 26, 2011 (hereby cancelled)
(j) DoD Manual 5105.21, Volumes 1 - 3, "Sensitive Compartmented Information (SCI) Administrative Security Manual," October 19, 2012
(k) DoD Manual 8910.01, Volume 1,"DoD Information Collections Manual: Procedures for DoD Internal Information Collections," June 30, 2014, as amended
(l) Section 2723 of title 10, United States Code
(m) DoD Directive 5210.50, "Management of Serious Security Incidents Involving Classified Information," October 27, 2014
(n) DoD Directive 5205.16, "The DoD Insider Threat Program," September 30, 2014, as amended
(o) Joint Under Secretary of Defense for Intelligence, DoD Chief Information Officer, and Commander, United States Strategic Command Memorandum, "Effective Integration of Cyber and Traditional Security Efforts," March 31, 2014
(p) DoD Directive 5111.1, "Under Secretary of Defense for Policy (USD(P))," December 8, 1999
(q) DoD Directive 5205.07, "Special Access Program (SAP) Policy," July 1, 2010
(r) DoD Inspector General Report DODIG-2013-142, "DoD Evaluation of Over-Classification of National Security Information," September 30, 2013
(s) DoD 5200.2-R, "Personnel Security Program," January 1987, as amended
(t) DoD Directive 5100.55, "United States Security Authority for North Atlantic Treaty Organization Affairs (USSAN)," February 27, 2006
(u) United States Security Authority for NATO Affairs Instruction 1-07, "Implementation of North Atlantic Treaty Organization (NATO) Security Requirements," April 5, 2007[1]
(v) DoD Directive 5230.09, "Clearance of DoD Information for Public Release," August 22, 2008, as amended
(w) DoD Instruction 5230.29, "Security and Policy Review of DoD Information for Public Release," August 13, 2014, as amended

[1] Available from the Central U.S. Registry.

(x) DoD Instruction 8550.01, "DoD Internet Services and Internet-Based Capabilities," September 11, 2012
(y) DoD Directive 5230.11, "Disclosure of Classified Military Information to Foreign Governments and International Organizations," June 16, 1992
(z) DoD Directive 5230.20, "Visits and Assignments of Foreign Nationals," June 22, 2005
(aa) DoD Instruction 5200.08, "Security of DoD Installations and Resources and the DoD Physical Security Review Board (PSRB)," December 10, 2005, as amended
(ab) DoD Instruction 5220.22, "National Industrial Security Program (NISP)," March 18, 2011
(ac) Executive Order 12968, "Access to Classified Information," August 2, 1995, as amended
(ad) Intelligence Community Directive 703, "Protection of Classified National intelligence, Including Sensitive Compartmental Information (SCI)," June 21 2013[2]
(ae) DoD Instruction 8500.01, "Cybersecurity," March 14, 2014
(af) Sections 3021, 3141, 3142, 3143, 3144, 1801(p) and 2673 of title 50, United States Code
(ag) Section 1011 of Public Law 108-458, "Intelligence Reform and Terrorism Prevention Act of 2004," December 17, 2004
(ah) Executive Order 12333, "United States Intelligence Activities," December 4, 1981, as amended
(ai) Part 1045 of title 10, Code of Federal Regulations
(aj) DoD Directive 5144.02, "DoD Chief Information Officer (DoD CIO),"November 21, 2014, as amended
(ak) National Security Directive 42, "National Policy for the Security of National Security Telecommunications and Information Systems," July 5, 1990[3]
(al) DoD Instruction 3305.13, "DoD Security Education, Training, and Certification," February 13, 2014
(an) National Security Agency/Central Security Service Policy Manual 3-16, "Control of Communications Security (COMSEC) Material," August 5, 2005[4]
(ao) DoD Instruction 1100.22, "Policy and Procedures for Determining Workforce Mix," April 12, 2010, as amended
(ap) Office of Federal Procurement Policy Letter 11-01, "Performance of Inherently Governmental and Critical Functions," September 12, 2011
(aq) Section 2011, et seq, of title 42, United States Code (also known as "The Atomic Energy Act of 1954, as amended")
(ar) DoD Directive 5210.48, "Credibility Assessment (CA) Program," April 24, 2015, as amended
(as) DoD Instruction 5210.02, "Access to and Dissemination of Restricted Data and Formerly Restricted Data," June 3, 2011, as amended
(at) DoD Instruction 5205.11, "Management, Administration, and Oversight of DoD Special Access Programs (SAPs)," February 6, 2013
(au) Chairman of the Joint Chiefs of Staff Instruction 3231.01B, "Safeguarding Nuclear Command and Control Extremely Sensitive Information," June 21, 2006[5]

---

[2] Available from the Office of the Director of National Intelligence.
[3] Available on SIPRNET at http://www.iad.nsa.smil.mil/resources/library/natl_pols_dirs_orders_section/index.cfm.
[4] CUI document, available to authorized users. Contact the NSA/CSS Office of Corporate Policy (DJP1) for assistance.
[5] This document is CUI. It is available to authorized recipients at https://ca.dtic.mil/cjcs_directives/index.htm

(av) Chapters 21, 22,[6] 31, 33, and 35 of title 44, United States Code
(aw) DoD Instruction 5015.02, "DoD Records Management Program," February 24, 2015, as amended
(ax) Sections 801-940 of title 10, United States Code (also known as "The Uniform Code of Military Justice")
(ay) Sections 102, 105, 552,[7] and 552a[8] of title 5, United States Code
(az) DoD Directive 5000.01, "The Defense Acquisition System," May 12, 2003
(ba) DoD Instruction 5000.02, "Operation of the Defense Acquisition System," January 7, 2015, as amended
(bb) DoD Instruction 5200.39, "Critical Program Information (CPI) Identification and Protection Within Research, Development, Test, and Evaluation (RDT&E)," May 28, 2015, as amended
(bc) DoD Instruction 3204.01, "DoD Policy for Oversight of Independent Research and Development (IR&D)," August 20, 2014
(bd) Sections 181 through 188 of title 35, United States Code (also known as "The Patent Secrecy Act of 1952, as amended")
(be) DoD Directive 5230.25, "Withholding of Unclassified Technical Data From Public Disclosure," November 6, 1984, as amended
(bf) Section 1041 of Public Law 106-65, "National Defense Authorization Act for Fiscal Year 2000," October 5, 1999
(bg) Section 3161 of Public Law 105-261, "Strom Thurmond National Defense Authorization Act for Fiscal Year 1999," October 17, 1998, as amended (also known as "The Kyl-Lott Amendment")
(bh) Presidential Memorandum, "Implementation of the Executive Order, 'Classified National Security Information,'" December 29, 2009
(bi) Executive Order 12951, "Release of Imagery Acquired by Space-Based National Intelligence Reconnaissance Systems," February 22, 1995
(bj) DoD 7000.14-R, Volume 11A, "Department of Defense Financial Management Regulation (FMR): Reimbursable Operations Policy," current edition
(bk) DoD Instruction 3200.12, "DoD Scientific and Technical Information Program (STIP)," August 22, 2013
(bl) Executive Order 12958, "Classified National Security Information," April 17, 1995, as amended
(bm) DoD Manual 5200.45, "Originating Classification Authority and Writing a Security Classification Guide," January 17, 2025

---

[6] Chapter 22 is also known as "The Presidential Records Act of 1978."
[7] Section 552 is also known as "The Freedom of Information Act, as amended."
[8] Section 552a is also known as "The Privacy Act of 1974, as amended."

ENCLOSURE 2

RESPONSIBILITIES

1. UNDER SECRETARY OF DEFENSE FOR INTELLIGENCE AND SECURITY (USD(I&S)). The USD(I&S) shall:

a. Serve as the DoD Senior Security Official, in accordance with Reference (a), and in that capacity is the DoD Senior Agency Official appointed pursuant to subsection 5.4(d) of Reference (d) to direct, administer, and oversee the DoD Information Security Program.

b. Notify the Congress and the Director, Information Security Oversight Office (ISOO), as appropriate, of violations involving classified information and of approval of waivers involving Reference (d) and its implementing directive, Reference (f), as required by section 2723 of title 10, United States Code (U.S.C.) (Reference (l)) and References (d) and (f).

c. Establish requirements for collecting and reporting data as necessary to fulfill the requirements of References (d) and (f) and other national-level guidance.

d. Designate a senior-level Federal employee, and an alternate, to represent the Department of Defense on the Interagency Security Classification Appeals Panel (ISCAP) as required by Reference (d). The individuals so designated must be full-time or permanent part-time employees of the Department of Defense. Designate to the ISCAP Chair in writing one or more individuals as identified by the Director, Washington Headquarters Services (WHS) to serve as a liaison in support of the DoD representative in accordance with the ISCAP bylaws in Reference (f).

e. Establish policy and oversee program implementation for reporting and investigating known or suspected incidents of unauthorized disclosure of classified information and for reporting corrective and disciplinary action taken in accordance with DoDD 5210.50 (Reference (m)).

f. Serve as the principal point of contact on counterintelligence (CI) and security investigative matters that involve the unauthorized disclosure of classified information referred to the Department of Defense by other government agencies or that may involve other government agencies in accordance with Reference (m).

g. Develop and oversee policy, strategy, plans, programs, required capabilities and resources for DoD intelligence, CI, security, sensitive activities, and other intelligence and security related matters, as necessary to counter insider threats. Serves as the senior official and principal advisor to the Secretary of Defense on the DoD Insider Threat program in accordance with DoDD 5205.16 (Reference (n)), and in this capacity, will:

(1) Provide oversight of the DoD Insider Threat Program.

(2) Assign responsibilities to the DoD Components to implement the DoD Insider Threat Program.

(3) Recommend improvements to the Secretary of Defense on DoD insider threat activities.

h. In coordination with the DoD Chief Information Officer (DoD CIO), the Chairman of the Joint Chiefs of Staff, the DoD Component heads, and the Director of National Intelligence, develop and integrate traditional and cyber security risk-based strategies and phased approaches to measurably increase DoD's security posture against insider threats in accordance with the joint USD(I&S), DoD CIO, and Commander, United States Strategic Command Memorandum (Reference (o)).

2. UNDER SECRETARY OF DEFENSE FOR POLICY (USD(P)). The USD(P) shall:

a. Serve as the senior official responsible for administering that portion of the DoD Information Security Program pertaining to the National Classified Military Information Disclosure Policy, foreign government (including North Atlantic Treaty Organization (NATO)) information, and security arrangements for international programs in accordance with DoDD 5111.1 (Reference (p)) and Reference (a).

b. Notify the Director, ISOO, of approval of waivers involving Reference (d) and its implementing directive, Reference (f).

3. DoD CIO. The DoD CIO shall:

a. Establish procedures, consistent with References (d) and (f) and this Manual, to ensure that information systems, including networks and telecommunications systems, that process, disseminate, or store classified information:

(1) Prevent access by unauthorized persons.

(2) Assure the integrity of the information.

(3) Use, to the maximum extent practicable, common information technology (IT) standards, protocols, and interfaces, and standardized electronic formats to maximize availability and authorized access.

b. Direct the use of technical means to prevent unauthorized copying of classified data and for anomaly detection to recognize unusual patterns of accessing, handling, downloading, and removal of digital classified information.

4. DIRECTOR, WHS. The Director, WHS, under the authority, direction, and control of the Chief Management Officer of the Department of Defense, through the Director of

Administration, shall identify to the USD(I&S) an individual and at least one alternate to serve as the ISCAP liaison for the Department of Defense in accordance with the ISCAP Bylaws in Reference (f).

5. HEADS OF THE DoD COMPONENTS. The Heads of the DoD Components shall, in accordance with Reference (b):

a. Be responsible for the overall management, functioning, and effectiveness of the information security program within their respective DoD Component.

b. Appoint a senior agency official to be responsible for directing, administering, and overseeing the information security program within the Component on his or her behalf and ensure that official accomplishes the responsibilities in section 7 of this enclosure. The DoD Component Head may designate a separate senior official to be responsible for overseeing SAPs within the Component, if necessary, in accordance with DoDD 5205.07 (Reference (q)).

c. If the Component is not an element of the Intelligence Community, designate a senior intelligence official to be responsible for ensuring adequate funding and effective implementation of the Component's SCI security program, including awareness and education, consistent with guidance established by the DNI.

d. Identify, program for, and commit necessary resources to effectively implement the requirements for protection of classified information as part of the Component's information security program.

e. Conduct, as periodically directed by the USD(I&S), reviews of the DoD Component's classification guidance and provide reports summarizing results.

f. Ensure the Component Senior Agency Official and the Component Senior Intelligence Official coordinate as appropriate to achieve a harmonized and cohesive information security program within the DoD Component.

6. SENIOR AGENCY OFFICIALS. The senior agency officials, under the authority, direction, and control of the Heads of the DoD Components, appointed in accordance with section 6 of this enclosure shall, in addition to the responsibilities in Volume 4 of this Manual:

a. Direct, administer, and oversee their respective DoD Component's information security program.

b. Develop guidance as necessary for program implementation within the DoD Component.

c. Direct the head of each activity within the DoD Component that creates, handles, or stores classified information to appoint, in writing, an official to serve as security manager for the activity, to properly manage and oversee the activity's information security program. Persons appointed to these positions shall be provided training as Enclosure 5 of Volume 3 of this Manual requires.

d. Establish and maintain an ongoing self-inspection and oversight program to evaluate and assess the effectiveness and efficiency of the DoD Component's implementation of that portion of the information security program pertaining to classified information.

(1) Evaluation criteria shall consider, at a minimum, original and derivative classification, declassification, safeguarding, security violations, education and training, and management and oversight.

(2) The program shall include regular review and assessment of representative samples of the DoD Component's classified products. Appropriate officials shall be authorized to correct misclassification of information, except for information covered by paragraph 17.b. or section 18 of Enclosure 4 of this Volume.

(3) Self-inspections shall be conducted at least annually with the frequency established based on program needs and classification activity. DoD Component activities that originate significant amounts of classified information should be inspected at least annually. Annual reports on the Component's self-inspection program shall be submitted as required by ISOO and/or USD(I&S). The report shall include:

(a) A description of the agency's self-inspection program, to include activities assessed, program areas covered, and methodology utilized.

(b) A summary of the findings in the following program areas: original classification, derivative classification, declassification, safeguarding, security violations, security education and training, and management and oversight.

(c) Specific information on the findings of the annual review of agency original and derivative classification actions to include the volume of classified materials reviewed and the number and type of discrepancies that were identified.

(d) Actions taken or planned to correct identified deficiencies or misclassification actions, and to deter their recurrence.

(e) Best practices identified. The DoD Inspector General Report DODIG-2013-142 (Reference (r)) identifies examples of DoD Component best practices, including the following:

(1) Using Microsoft SharePoint to make available all information that security managers need to manage their programs and share unit best practices.

(2) Creating and using an electronic security manager handbook.

(3) Providing and maintaining open communications between different levels of management structure within the organization.

(4) Establishing and using online training tools to track training requirement completion.

(5) Issuing and using the Quarterly Security newsletter that provides information security articles, security updates, and upcoming security courses.

(6) Maintaining an automated security incident reporting program.

(7) Maintaining complete inventories of all classified documents and electronic media to provide precise tracking of classified holdings.

(8) Developing organization derivative classification training.

(9) Reviewing the process for public release of information.

(10) Maintaining a central security and education awareness mailbox with questions answered by close of business.

(11) Tracking mandatory annual security and derivative classification training by the Human Resources Information System of Record, which enhances better oversight of training completion rates.

(12) Developing a comprehensive security database reflecting final adjudication and investigation of security incidents.

e. Establish procedures to prevent unauthorized persons from accessing classified information, including:

(1) Specific requirements for protecting classified information at DoD Component-sponsored meetings and conferences, to include seminars, exhibits, symposiums, conventions, training activities, workshops, or other such gatherings, during which classified information is disseminated.

(2) Requirements for protecting U.S. classified information located in foreign countries, with particular attention on ensuring proper enforcement of controls on release of U.S. classified information to foreign entities.

(3) Procedures to accommodate visits to DoD Component facilities involving access to, or disclosure of, classified information.

f. Establish and maintain declassification programs and plans that meet the requirements of this Manual and ensure that necessary resources are applied to the review of information to ensure it is neither classified for longer than necessary nor declassified prematurely.

g. Establish and maintain a security education and training program as required by Enclosure 5 of Volume 3 of this Manual, ensure that DoD Component personnel receive security education and training as appropriate to their functions, and grant, when appropriate, waivers to the original and derivative classification training requirements of section 7 of Enclosure 5 of Volume 3.

h. Ensure that the performance contract or other system used to rate the performance of civilian and military personnel includes the designation and management of classified information, to include Restricted Data and Formerly Restricted Data information when appropriate, as a critical element or item to be evaluated in the rating of:

(1) OCAs.

(2) Security managers and security specialists.

(3) Personnel who derivatively classify information on a routine basis.

(4) Information system security personnel if their duties involve access to classified information and information system personnel (e.g., system administrators) with privileged access to classified system or network resources.

(5) All other personnel whose duties include significant involvement with the creation or handling of classified information.

i. Account for the costs associated with implementing this Manual within the DoD Component and report those costs as required.

j. Ensure prompt and appropriate response to any request, appeal, challenge, complaint, or suggestion arising out of implementation of this Manual within the DoD Component.

k. Establish procedures for receipt of information, allegations, or complaints regarding over-classification or incorrect classification within the DoD Component and, as needed, provide guidance to personnel on proper classification.

l. Approve, when appropriate, the use of alternative compensatory control measures (ACCM) for classified information over which the senior agency official has cognizance and provide written notification within 30 days to the Director of Security, Office of the Under Secretary of Defense for Intelligence and Security (OUSD(I&S)), or the Director, International Security Programs, Defense Technology Security Administration, Office of the USD(P) (OUSD(P)), as appropriate, when establishing or terminating an ACCM.

m. Submit an annual report addressing how the DoD Component implemented that portion of the information security program dealing with classified information.

(1) The report, covering the previous fiscal year, shall be submitted on Standard Form (SF) 311, "Agency Information Security Program Data," to reach the Director of Security,

OUSD(I&S), prior to October 31 of each year. The Military Departments shall submit their reports directly to ISOO, with a copy furnished to OUSD(I&S). OUSD(I&S) shall compile the reports, excluding those of the Military Departments, and provide a consolidated report to ISOO.

(2) The SF 311 shall be completed according to the instructions accompanying the form and those provided by ISOO and OUSD(I&S).

n. Cooperate and coordinate with the Component senior intelligence official as appropriate to achieve a harmonized and cohesive information security program within the DoD Component.

7. HEADS OF DoD ACTIVITIES. The heads of DoD activities shall:

a. Be responsible for overall management, functioning and effectiveness of the activity's information security program.

b. Designate, in writing, an activity security manager, who shall be given the necessary authority to ensure personnel adhere to program requirements. Provide the designated activity security manager direct access to activity leadership and ensure he or she is organizationally aligned to ensure prompt and appropriate attention to program requirements.

(1) The activity security manager may be assigned full-time, part-time, or as a collateral duty, provided that the responsibilities delineated in section 9 of this enclosure can be adequately and professionally executed and implemented.

(2) The activity security manager shall:

(a) Be a military officer, senior non-commissioned officer, or a civilian employee with sufficient authority, staff, and other resources necessary to manage the program for the activity.

1. For activities with more than 100 personnel assigned, a senior non-commissioned officer designated as the activity security manager shall be E-7 or above; a civilian employee so designated shall be GS-11 or above (or pay band equivalent).

2. For activities with less than 100 personnel assigned, a senior non-commissioned officer designated as the activity security manager shall be E-6 or above; a civilian employee so designated shall be GS-7 or above (or pay band equivalent).

(b) Be a U.S. citizen.

(c) Have been the subject of a favorably adjudicated, current background investigation appropriate for the highest level of classification of information handled by personnel within the activity in accordance with requirements of DoD 5200.2-R (Reference (s)).

(d) Have access appropriate to the level of information managed.

c. In large activities and where circumstances warrant, designate, in writing, activity assistant security manager(s) to assist in program implementation, maintenance, and local oversight.

(1) Responsibilities assigned to assistant security managers shall be commensurate with their grade level, experience, and training.

(2) Individuals assigned as assistant security managers shall be U.S. citizens with security clearances and accesses appropriate to their assigned responsibilities.

(3) Assistant security managers shall report directly to the activity security manager who shall provide guidance, direction, coordination, training, and oversight necessary to ensure that the program is being administered effectively.

d. Optionally, where circumstances warrant (such as in activities with large repositories of Top Secret information), designate an activity Top Secret control officer (TSCO) to manage and account for Top Secret materials, and Top Secret control assistant(s) (TSCA(s)) as needed to assist the TSCO. When used, designations shall be in writing. Top Secret couriers are NOT considered TSCA(s).

(1) An individual designated as the TSCO must have been the subject of a favorably adjudicated, current background investigation in accordance with requirements of Reference (s) and must have Top Secret access. The TSCO shall report directly to the activity security manager, or the activity security manager may serve concurrently as the TSCO.

(2) An individual designated as a TSCA must have been the subject of a favorably adjudicated, current background investigation in accordance with requirements of Reference (s) and must have Top Secret access.

e. When required by DoDD 5100.55 (Reference (t)), designate, in writing, an activity NATO control point officer and at least one alternate to ensure that NATO information is correctly controlled and accounted for, and that NATO security procedures are followed. United States Security Authority for NATO (USSAN) Instruction 1-07 (Reference (u)) was written by USD(P) on behalf of the Secretary of Defense, acting as the U.S. Security Authority to NATO and administrator of NATO information security regulation. It establishes procedures and minimum security standards for the handling and protection of NATO classified information.

8. ACTIVITY SECURITY MANAGER. The activity security manager shall:

a. Manage and implement the DoD activity's information security program on behalf of the activity head, to whom he or she shall have direct access.

b. Serve as the principal advisor and representative to the activity head in all matters pertaining to this Manual and maintain cognizance of all activity information, personnel, information systems, physical and industrial security functions to ensure that the information security program is coordinated in its execution and inclusive of all requirements in this Manual.

c. Provide guidance, direction, coordination, and oversight to designated assistant security managers, TSCOs, TSCAs, security assistants and, as appropriate, others in security management roles as necessary to ensure that all elements of the information security program are being administered effectively, efficiently, and in a coordinated manner.

d. Develop a written activity security instruction that shall include provisions for safeguarding classified information during emergency situations and military operations, if appropriate.

e. Ensure that personnel in the activity who perform security duties are kept abreast of changes in policies and procedures, and provide assistance in solving problems.

f. Formulate, coordinate, and conduct the activity security education and training program. Organizations with elements that are deployable for contingency operations shall ensure information security training, to include appropriate application to information systems, is an integral part of pre-deployment training and preparation.

g. Ensure that threats to security and security incidents pertaining to classified information, including foreign government information (FGI), are reported, recorded, coordinated with the proper authorities, and, when necessary, investigated and that appropriate action is taken to mitigate damage and prevent recurrence. Ensure that incidents involving the loss or compromise of classified material (as described in Enclosure 6 of Volume 3 of this Manual) are immediately referred to the cognizant investigative authority. In cases where compromise is determined or cannot be ruled out, ensure that security reviews and other required assessments are conducted as soon as possible. Coordinate with local information assurance officials, but retain responsibility for inquiries into incidents involving possible or actual compromise of classified information resident in or on IT systems.

h. Coordinate the preparation, dissemination, and maintenance of security classification guides under the activity's cognizance as required by Reference (bm).

i. Maintain liaison with the activity public affairs officer or information security officer, as appropriate, and the operations security (OPSEC) officer to ensure that information, including press releases and photos, proposed or intended for public release, including via website posting, is subject to a security review in accordance with DoDD 5230.09 (Reference (v)), DoDI 5230.29 (Reference (w)), and DoDI 8550.01 (Reference (x)).

j. Coordinate with other activity officials regarding security measures for the classification, safeguarding, transmission, declassification, and destruction of classified information.

(1) Coordinate as required with the foreign disclosure officer on all matters governing the disclosure of classified information to foreign governments and international organizations in accordance with DoDD 5230.11 (Reference (y)).

(2) Ensure implementation of and compliance with the requirements of this Manual for all uses of IT. Coordinate with information systems security personnel (e.g., designated approval authorities (DAAs), information assurance managers (IAMs), information system security managers) as required for effective management, use, and oversight of classified information in electronic form.

k. Develop security measures and procedures, consistent with DoDD 5230.20 (Reference (z)), DoDI 5200.08 (Reference (aa)) and other applicable policies, regarding visitors who require access to classified information and facilities containing same.

l. Ensure compliance with the requirements of this Manual when access to classified information is provided to industry at activity facilities and locations in connection with a classified contract. If the classified information is provided to industry at the contractor's facility, ensure compliance with the provisions of DoDI 5220.22 (Reference (ab)).

m. Ensure that access to classified information is limited to appropriately cleared personnel with a need to know as required by section 4.1 of Reference (d) and section 3.1 of E.O. 12968 (Reference (ac)).

n. Maintain liaison with the special security officer (SSO), as appropriate, on issues of common concern.

9. TSCO. The TSCO, when designated in accordance with paragraph 8.d. of this enclosure, shall:

a. For paper documents and other physical media (e.g., disk drives and removable computer media), maintain a system of accountability (e.g., registry) to record the receipt, reproduction, transfer, transmission, downgrading, declassification, and destruction of Top Secret information, that is not SAP, SCI, and other special types of classified information.

b. Ensure that inventories of Top Secret information are conducted at least annually or more frequently when circumstances warrant.

10. SENIOR INTELLIGENCE OFFICIALS. The senior intelligence officials, including those who are heads of elements of the Intelligence Community and those designated according to paragraph 6.c of this enclosure, shall:

a. In accordance with Reference (b):

(1) Protect intelligence and intelligence sources and methods from unauthorized disclosure consistent with the policies of the DNI and, where applicable, the requirements of this Manual and Reference (j).

(2) Administer and oversee, within their respective organizations, those aspects of the SCI security programs not delegated to Defense Intelligence Agency (DIA) in accordance with Reference (b).

(3) Develop DoD Component-specific implementation guidance as necessary for the protection of SCI.

b. Cooperate and coordinate with the Component senior agency official as appropriate to achieve a harmonized and cohesive information security program within the DoD Component.

c. Where required by this Manual, provide the USD(I&S) with copies of requests for exceptions and waivers of information security policies, security incident reports, and other information submitted to the DNI.

d. Designate, as required by Intelligence Community Directive 703 (Reference (ad)) and Reference (j), an activity SSO to be responsible for the day-to-day security management, operation, implementation, use, and dissemination of SCI within the activity and, as needed, alternate SSO(s). Such designations shall be made for any activity that is accredited for and authorized to receive, use, and store SCI and shall be in writing.

(1) All SCI matters shall be referred to the SSO.

(2) The SSO may be designated as the activity security manager if the grade requirements for the position are met; however, the activity security manager cannot function as the SSO unless so designated by the cognizant senior intelligence official.

11. INFORMATION SYSTEMS SECURITY OFFICIALS. Information systems security officials (e.g., DAA or agency official (AO), IAM or information systems security manager (ISSM), and information systems security officer) designated, in writing, as required by DoDI 8500.01 (Reference (ae)), shall:

a. Coordinate with the activity security manager regarding implementation of information systems security measures and procedures.

b. Notify the activity security manager, who retains overall security responsibility for required inquiries and investigations, when there are incidents involving possible or actual compromise or data spills of classified information resident in information systems, as required by Reference (ae), and coordinate with him or her as required for resolution of the incident.

ENCLOSURE 3

DoD INFORMATION SECURITY PROGRAM OVERVIEW

1. PURPOSE. Effective execution of a robust information security program that gives equal priority to both protecting information and demonstrating a commitment to open Government and that includes accurate, accountable application of classification standards and routine, secure, and effective declassification is a national security imperative. This Manual provides overarching program guidance and direction for the DoD Information Security Program. While day-to-day program execution is the responsibility of all DoD personnel, program implementation must be guided by active and engaged senior managers at all levels who have the responsibility for overall program execution and by security managers who ensure the program is visible, effective, and efficient.

2. SCOPE. The DoD Information Security Program implements References (b), (d), and (f) with regard to the classification, declassification, and protection of classified information, including information categorized as collateral, SCI, and SAP, and provides guidance to users to identify, mark, and protect certain types of unclassified information, referred to as CUI, in accordance with Reference (e), Reference (f), and other national-level directives. This combined guidance is known as the DoD Information Security Program and is applicable to all DoD Components.

3. PERSONAL RESPONSIBILITY. All personnel of the Department of Defense are personally and individually responsible for properly protecting classified information and CUI under their custody and control. All officials within the Department of Defense who hold command, management, or supervisory positions have specific, non-delegable responsibility for the quality and effectiveness of implementation and management of the information security program within their areas of responsibility.

4. NATIONAL AUTHORITIES FOR SECURITY MATTERS

a. President of the United States. The President of the United States bears executive responsibility for the security of the Nation, which includes the authority to classify information for the protection of the national defense and foreign relations of the United States. The President has established standards for the classification, safeguarding, and declassification of national security information through the issuance of Reference (d) and for the designation and protection of CUI through the issuance of Reference (e).

b. National Security Council (NSC). In accordance with section 3021 of title 50, U.S.C. (Reference (af)), the NSC provides overall policy guidance on information security.

c. DNI. The DNI is head of the Intelligence Community and principal advisor to the President and the NSC for intelligence matters related to national security pursuant to Section 1011 of Public Law 108-458 (Reference (ag)) and Section 1.3 of E.O. 12333 (Reference (ah)). The DNI is also charged by section 1.3(b)(8) of Reference (ah) with protecting intelligence sources, methods, and activities, and in this role, the DNI issues instructions in the form of Intelligence Community Directives or other security policies and standards for the protection, management and oversight of SCI and other national intelligence.

d. ISOO. The ISOO, under the authority of the Archivist of the United States, acting in consultation with the NSC, issues directives as necessary to implement Reference (d). The directives establish national standards for the classification and marking of national security information, security education and training programs, safeguarding, self-inspection programs, and declassification. The ISOO has the responsibility to oversee agency implementation and compliance with these directives. In this role, the ISOO requests certain information regarding DoD activities, and such requests are coordinated through USD(I&S).

e. CUI Office (CUIO). The CUIO, under the authority of the Archivist of the United States, issues directives as necessary to implement Reference (e). The directives establish national standards for designation, safeguarding, marking, and dissemination of CUI as well as standards for education and training. The CUIO has the responsibility to oversee agency implementation and compliance with these directives. CUIO requests for information regarding DoD activities are coordinated through USD(I&S).

5. DoD INFORMATION SECURITY PROGRAM MANAGEMENT

a. USD(I&S). Reference (a) designates the USD(I&S) as the DoD Senior Security Official. In this role, the USD(I&S) is the DoD Senior Agency Official responsible for directing, administering, and overseeing the DoD Information Security Program for the Department of Defense, and except as provided in paragraph 5.b. of this section, performs the functions specified in subsection 5.4(d) of Reference (d) and its implementing directives for the Department of Defense. The USD(I&S) is also the Restricted Data Management Official for the Department of Defense consistent with the requirement in part 1045 of title 10, Code of Federal Regulations (References (ai) and (as)).

b. USD(P). In accordance with Reference (p), the USD(P) is the senior official responsible for directing, administering, and overseeing that portion of the DoD Information Security Program pertaining to foreign government (including NATO) information, the disclosure of classified information to foreign governments and international organizations, and security arrangements for international programs. Within the scope of these responsibilities, the USD(P) also performs the functions specified in subsection 5.4(d) of Reference (d) and its implementing directives for the Department of Defense.

c. DoD CIO. In accordance with DoDD 5144.02 (Reference (aj)), the DoD CIO is responsible for all matters relating to the DoD information enterprise, including communications; spectrum management; network policy and standards; information systems; cybersecurity;

positioning, navigation, and timing policy; and the DoD information enterprise that supports DoD command and control.

d. National Security Agency/Central Security Service (NSA/CSS). In accordance with Reference (ah), the NSA/CSS provides centralized coordination and direction for signals intelligence. In accordance with National Security Directive 42 (Reference (ak)), the NSA/CSS provides IA/cybersecurity support for national security systems and, at the request of the national security system owner, provides vulnerability assessments. Additionally, in accordance with Reference (b), the Director, NSA/Chief, CSS may impose special requirements for protection of classified cryptologic information.

e. DIA. As assigned by Reference (b) and with the exception of NSA/CSS, the National Reconnaissance Office, and the National Geospatial-Intelligence Agency, DIA administers within the Department of Defense the SCI security policies and procedures issued by the DNI. The Director, DIA, is responsible for development of standards, implementation, and operational management of the SCI compartments for the Department of Defense.

f. Defense Security Service (DSS). DSS provides information security education and training for the Department of Defense as required by DoDI 3305.13 (Reference (al)). DSS, as the DoD cognizant security office for industrial security, also manages and administers the DoD portion of the National Industrial Security Program, to ensure the protection of classified information released or disclosed to industry in connection with classified contracts.

6. DoD COMPONENT INFORMATION SECURITY MANAGEMENT

a. Head of the DoD Component. The Head of each DoD Component has overall responsibility for implementation of the information security program within the Component. This includes responsibility for:

(1) Designating senior agency officials, including, as appropriate, the DoD Component senior agency official and senior intelligence official, to be responsible for directing, administering, and overseeing the information security program within the Component. A separate senior official responsible for overseeing SAPs within the Component may also be designated.

(2) Committing necessary resources to effectively implement the information security program.

b. Senior Agency Officials. The senior agency official appointed by the Head of the DoD Component has day-to-day responsibility for the direction, implementation, and oversight of Component's information security program and for its efficient and effective implementation. These responsibilities include:

(1) Promulgating guidance necessary for program implementation.

(2) Ensuring adequate resources for a robust information security program are identified and programmed.

(3) Establishing and maintaining a security education program.

(4) Establishing and maintaining an ongoing self-inspection and program oversight function.

(5) Directing the head of each activity within the DoD Component that creates, handles, or stores classified information to appoint an official to serve as security manager for the activity, to properly manage and oversee the activity's information security program.

c. Activity Security Management. The activity security manager manages and implements the activity's information security program and ensures its visibility and effectiveness on behalf of the activity head, who retains the responsibility for overall management and functioning of the program. The activity security managers must have sufficient delegated authority to ensure that personnel adhere to program requirements, and their position within the organizational hierarchy must ensure their credibility and enable them to raise security issues directly to their respective activity head.

(1) Some tasks may be assigned to a number of activity personnel and may even be assigned to persons senior to the security manager. Nevertheless, the security manager shall remain cognizant of all activity information, personnel, information systems, and physical and industrial security functions, and shall ensure that the information security program is coordinated and inclusive of all requirements in this Manual.

(2) The activity security manager responsibilities include:

(a) Serving as the principal advisor and representative to the activity head in all matters pertaining to this Manual.

(b) Developing a written activity security instruction.

(c) Ensuring that personnel in the activity who perform security duties are trained.

(d) Formulating, coordinating, and conducting the activity security education program.

d. TSCO. TSCOs are not required, but the activity head may elect to appoint a TSCO to facilitate appropriate control of Top Secret material when there is a need (e.g., accountability of Sigma 14 material as required in Volume 2 of this Manual). The TSCO maintains, for paper and other physical media (e.g., disk drives and removable computer media), a system of accountability (e.g., a registry) for activity Top Secret information and conducts inventories of Top Secret information.

(1) When collateral Top Secret information is maintained in a sensitive compartmented information facility (SCIF) or SAP secure facility, it may be handled in the same manner as SCI and SAP materials once necessary receipts have been provided to the organization supplying the materials. When collateral Top Secret material is taken out of a SCIF or SAP secure facility it shall be reentered into the registry system for accountability.

(2) Repositories, libraries, or activities that store large volumes of classified documents may limit their annual inventory to that which access has been given in the past 12 months, and 10 percent of the remaining inventory.

(3) Accountability for Top Secret SCI, SAP, and other special types of classified information shall be in accordance with References (j) through (y), and other applicable guidance.

e. Other Security Management Roles

(1) Assistant Security Manager. In large activities and where circumstances warrant, activities may designate U.S. Government civilian or military members as assistant security manager(s) to assist the activity security manager with program implementation, maintenance, and local oversight.

(2) Security Assistants. As warranted, activities may assign U.S. Government civilian, military members, or contractor employees as security assistants to perform administrative security functions under the direction of the activity security manager without regard for job series or title or for rank, rate, or grade as long as they have the clearance required for the access needed to perform their assigned duties and tasks. (While the scope of responsibilities and job titles covered by the General Schedule (GS) 0086 Security Clerical and Assistance Series can be consistent with the duties of a security assistant as described in this paragraph, the role of security assistant as described in this paragraph does not require that civilian employees hold this job series.)

(3) Communication Security (COMSEC) Custodian. The COMSEC Custodian is the activity head's primary advisor on matters concerning the security and handling of COMSEC information and hardware and the associated records and reports and functions in accordance with NSA/CSS Policy Manual 3-16 (Reference (an)).

(4) NATO Control Point Officer. In accordance with Reference (t), the Secretary of the Army operates the Central U.S. Registry (CUSR), the main receiving and dispatching element for NATO information in the U.S. Government. The activity NATO Control Point Officer and any designated alternate(s) ensure that NATO information is correctly controlled and accounted for and that NATO security procedures specified in Reference (u) are followed. The CUSR manages the U.S. Registry system of subregistries, communications centers, and control points to maintain accountability of NATO classified information and it conducts inspections of the associated security processes and procedures. Further information can be found at http://www.cusr.army.mil.

(5) SSO. An SSO is to be designated by the Senior Intelligence Official for any activity that is accredited for and authorized to receive, use, and store SCI. The activity SSO is responsible, in accordance with References (j) and (ad), for the day-to-day security management, operation, implementation, use, and dissemination of SCI within the activity.

(6) SAP Security Officer. In accordance with the requirements of Reference (q), a SAP security officer is to be designated for any activity that is accredited for and authorized to receive, use, and store SAP information.

(7) Information Systems Security Officials. Information systems security officials (e.g., AO, ISSM, and information systems security officer) manage and oversee the DoD IT infrastructure (i.e., computer systems and networks). As computers are found everywhere within the Department of Defense, close coordination with these officials regarding implementation of security measures and procedures is imperative.

(8) CI and OPSEC. The activity's information security program must also be closely coordinated and aligned with the DoD Component's CI and OPSEC functions in order to maintain the security essential to warfighter and mission success.

7. USE OF CONTRACTORS IN SECURITY ADMINISTRATION. In accordance with DoDI 1100.22 (Reference (ao)) and Office of Federal Procurement Policy Letter 11-01 (Reference (ap)), there are certain critical, closely associated with inherently governmental, or otherwise exempt functions and activities that cannot or should not be performed by a contractor. The DoD Components shall be careful not to outsource security functions that are inherently governmental.

a. Activity security management shall ensure that contractors who are involved in security administration and support duties are clearly identified in their capacities, roles, and functions, to ensure there is no possible confusion regarding which security personnel may exercise inherently governmental authorities and which may not.

b. Inherently governmental activities and functions include those that require either the exercise of substantial discretion in applying U.S. Government authority, or value judgments when making decisions for the U.S. Government. Inherently governmental security functions include, but are not limited to:

(1) Approving and issuing security policies and procedures.

(2) Making original classification decisions, or rendering classification determinations regarding classified information that is improperly or incompletely marked. (Correcting improper markings when the appropriate classification is not in question is not considered rendering a classification determination.)

(3) Deciding to downgrade or declassify information. (Adhering to security markings on information or to guidance stated in an appropriate security classification or declassification guide is not considered a downgrading or declassification decision.)

(4) Deciding challenges to classification and any appeals.

(5) Making foreign disclosure decisions pursuant to Reference (y).

(6) Making public release decisions pursuant to Reference (v).

(7) Committing to expenditure of U.S. Government funds pursuant to References ((ao) and (ap)).

(8) Conducting investigations of, or determining fault in, security incidents involving U.S. Government or other contractor personnel. (Contractors may conduct preliminary inquiries to determine if a security incident is a violation or an infraction.)

(9) Giving final approval or executing documents for filing in litigation if documents assert an official position of the Department of Defense, any DoD Component, or any other Federal agency.

8. USE OF FOREIGN NATIONALS IN SECURITY ADMINISTRATION. Foreign nationals may not engage in the following DoD security administrative activities:

a. Approving and issuing security policies and procedures.

b. Making original classification decisions, or rendering classification determinations regarding classified information that is improperly or incompletely marked. Correcting improper markings when the appropriate classification is not in question is not considered rendering a classification determination.

c. Deciding to downgrade or declassify information. Adhering to security markings on information or guidance stated in an appropriate security classification or declassification guide is not considered a downgrading or declassification decision.

d. Deciding challenges to classification or any appeals.

e. Making foreign disclosure decisions pursuant to Reference (y).

f. Making public release decisions pursuant to Reference (v).

g. Committing to expenditure of U.S. Government funds. Guidelines within international or host nation agreements or treaties may provide exceptions to this area of security administration.

h. Conducting investigations of, or determining fault in, security incidents involving U.S. Government or contractor personnel.

i. Giving final approval or executing documents for filing in litigation, if documents assert an official position of the Department of Defense, any DoD Component, or any other federal agency.

j. Escorting personnel, except where the foreign national is employed by DoD and the foreign national escorts personnel:

(1) As a specific function of his or her assigned duties.

(2) Only to areas where U.S. personnel are embedded within locations or facilities that are outside the continental United States.

(3) Only in situations not detrimental to the interests of the DoD or the U.S. Government.

k. Accessing combinations at the entrance and exit doors or security containers that contain non-releasable classified information or non-releasable CUI.

l. Accessing codes or functions associated with the intrusion detection system or master codes associated with access control devices.

m. Accessing IT equipment, such as computers, printers, or fax equipment used to process non-releasable classified information or non-releasable CUI.

n. Constructing or modifying areas where classified information will be processed, unless cleared U.S. national civil engineers provide oversight to all new construction and modifications of facilities where classified information will be processed.

o. Accessing SCIFs, except as stated in Volume 2 of Reference (j).

9. CLASSIFICATION AUTHORITY. Except for information subject to section 2011 et seq., of title 42, U.S.C. (also known and hereinafter referred to as "The Atomic Energy Act of 1954, as amended" (Reference (aq)), Reference (d) and this Manual provide the only authority for applying security classification to information within the Department of Defense.

10. CLASSIFICATION POLICY. Information shall be classified only when necessary in the interests of national security and shall be declassified as soon as is consistent with the requirements of national security.

11. RECLASSIFICATION. After information has been declassified and released to the public under proper authority, it may be reclassified only in accordance with paragraph 17.b. of Enclosure 4.

12. ACCESS TO CLASSIFIED INFORMATION

a. Requirements for Access. Persons shall be allowed access to classified information only if they:

(1) Possess a valid and appropriate security clearance in accordance with Reference (s). Reference (s) contains detailed guidance on personnel security investigation, adjudication, and clearance.

(2) Have executed an appropriate non-disclosure agreement.

(3) Have a valid need to know the information in order to perform a lawful and authorized governmental function.

b. Nondisclosure Agreements

(1) Before being granted access to Confidential, Secret, or Top Secret information, employees shall sign SF 312, "Classified Information Nondisclosure Agreement," or other non-disclosure agreement approved by the DNI. SF 312 (or its predecessor, SF 189), or a legally enforceable facsimile retained in lieu of the original, shall be maintained for 50 years from the date of signature. Electronic signatures shall not be used to execute the SF 312.

(2) Before being granted access to SCI information, individuals adjudicated and approved for access shall sign a DNI-authorized SCI nondisclosure agreement. Consistent with the provisions of DoDD 5210.48 (Reference (ar)) and all applicable laws, that agreement shall include, as an addendum, the individual's written certification that they may be asked to undergo a polygraph examination in connection with any investigation of an unauthorized disclosure of SCI information to which they have had access.

(3) Before being granted access to SAP information, individuals adjudicated and approved for access shall additionally sign a DoD-approved program indoctrination agreement(s) for that information as required by Reference (q). Before gaining access and during a period of access to DoD SAPs, all personnel shall consent to, and be subject to, a random CI-scope polygraph examination as required by Reference (q).

c. NATO Briefing for Cleared Personnel. To facilitate potential access to NATO classified information, all DoD military and civilian personnel who are briefed on their responsibilities for protecting U.S. classified information shall be briefed simultaneously on the requirements for protecting NATO information. A written acknowledgement of the individual's receipt of the NATO briefing and responsibilities for safeguarding NATO classified information shall be maintained. As stipulated in Reference (u), access to NATO classified information shall also require a supervisor's determination of the individual's need to know and possession of the requisite security clearance. Receipt of the NATO briefing shall be verified prior to granting access to NATO classified information.

d. Access By Individuals Outside the Executive Branch. See section 6, Enclosure 2 of Volume 3 of this Manual for further guidance regarding access to classified information by individuals outside the Executive Branch.

13. PROTECTION REQUIREMENTS. Classified information and CUI shall be protected at all times. Volumes 1 through 3 of this Manual provide guidance for the protection of classified information while Volume 4 provides guidance for the protection of CUI. Additional guidance for special types of information is provided by this section.

a. Protection of Restricted Data (RD) and Formerly Restricted Data (FRD). Classified information, including Critical Nuclear Weapon Design Information (CNWDI), in the custody of the Department of Defense marked as RD or FRD in accordance with the Atomic Energy Act of 1954, as amended, shall be stored, protected, and destroyed as this Manual requires for other information of a comparable level of security classification.

(1) Consult DoDI 5210.02 (Reference (as)) for DoD policy and procedures concerning access to and dissemination of RD, FRD, and CNWDI within the Department of Defense. Reference (as) also provides guidance on access, distribution, handling, and accountability of Sigma information.

(2) Until DoD public key infrastructure is generally deployed on the Secret Internet Protocol Router Network (SIPRNET), the following security measures, deemed sufficient to provide the access and dissemination controls required by Reference (as), shall be implemented when processing RD and CNWDI on SIPRNET:

(a) RD and CNWDI shall be e-mailed only after confirmation that the recipient has a final security clearance at the appropriate level, has a need to know the information, and, for CNWDI, has received the additional security briefing required by Reference (as).

(b) All RD and CNWDI files stored on shared or personal local electronic storage devices shall be password-protected.

(c) IT systems and networks must be certified and accredited for RD, FRD, and/or CNWDI prior to transmission, processing, or storage of such data. Such certification must verify that access to RD, FRD, and CNWDI information, including through websites, is limited to authorized recipients by, at a minimum, a properly administered and protected individual identifier and password consistent with requirements of Reference (ae).

(d) System log-ons and properly configured screen savers are sufficient protection for e-mail files.

(e) In accordance with Reference (as), Sigma 14, 15, and 20 information shall not be processed on SIPRNET.

b. Protection of SCI. SCI information shall be controlled and protected in accordance with applicable national policy, policies established by the DNI, and implementing DoD issuances. Security classification and declassification policies of this Manual apply to SCI information in the same manner as other classified information.

c. Protection of COMSEC Information. COMSEC information shall be controlled and protected in accordance with applicable national policy and DoD issuances. Security classification and declassification policies of this Manual apply to COMSEC information in the same manner as other classified information, except ONLY NSA/CSS is authorized to declassify COMSEC information.

d. Protection of SAP Information. SAPs shall be created, continued, managed, and discontinued in accordance with Reference (q) and DoDI 5205.11 (Reference (at)). Information covered by SAPs established in accordance with References (q) and (at) shall be classified, declassified, controlled, and protected as this Manual, References (q) and (at), and instructions issued by officials charged with management of those programs require. The provisions of this Manual pertaining to classification, declassification, and marking apply, without exception, to SAP information unless waivers of specific requirements are obtained in accordance with section 16 of this enclosure.

e. Protection of NATO and FGI. NATO classified information shall be safeguarded consistent with References (d) and (u). Other FGI shall be safeguarded consistent with Reference (d) and the requirements of this Manual, except as required by the Appendix to Enclosure 4 of Volume 3; treaties; or international agreements. Information that is jointly developed with a foreign partner under a cooperative program agreement will be safeguarded in accordance with the security and disclosure provisions of the cooperative arrangement.

f. Protection of Nuclear Command and Control-Extremely Sensitive Information (NC2-ESI). Certain information pertaining to the command and control of nuclear weapons is designated NC2-ESI. NC2-ESI information shall be marked, safeguarded, and distributed in accordance with CJCS Instruction 3231.01B (Reference (au)).

14. RETENTION. Classified information and CUI shall be maintained only when it is required for effective and efficient operation of the organization or if law, treaty, international agreement, or regulation requires its retention. Such information shall be disposed in accordance with the provisions of chapter 33 of title 44, U.S.C. (Reference (av)), as implemented by DoDD 5015.02 (Reference (aw)), and DoD Component implementing directives and records schedules.

15. PERMANENTLY VALUABLE RECORDS. Classified and controlled unclassified documents and material that constitute permanently valuable records of the U.S. Government shall be maintained and disposed of in accordance with Reference (aw) and appropriate DoD

Component directives and records schedules. Other classified and controlled unclassified material shall be destroyed as specified in this Manual. When transferring classified records for storage or archival purposes to the National Archives and Records Administration (NARA) or to other locations, identify the boxes that contain foreign government documents as well as DoD documents containing FGI.

16. MILITARY OPERATIONS. Military commanders may modify the provisions of this Manual pertaining to accountability, dissemination, transmission, and storage of classified and controlled unclassified material and information as necessary to meet local conditions encountered during military operations. Military operations include combat and peacekeeping operations but not routine Military deployments or exercises. Classified information and CUI shall be introduced into combat areas or zones, or areas of potential hostile activity, only as necessary to accomplish the military mission.

17. WAIVERS AND EXCEPTIONS. Unless otherwise specified in this Volume, the DoD Components must submit requests for information security waivers or exceptions to the standards and requirements in this Manual through the chain of command to the USD(I&S), Attn: Director, Security Policy and Oversight Division, for approval.

a. If the waiver or exception involves any of the other security areas (e.g., industrial, physical, personnel), it must first be internally coordinated with the applicable security office(s) before the waiver or exception request is submitted for endorsement by the senior agency official (SAO). This may involve a separate request for waiver or exception based on the requirements of the other security policy issuances.

b. Waivers or exceptions pertaining to foreign government (including NATO) information and security arrangements for international programs must only be submitted to and approved by the USD(P), who will ensure concurrence by the USD(I&S) if the request involves the any of the security disciplines.

c. The Military Departments will forward requests for waiver or exception through their SAOs for endorsement before submitting such requests to the USD(I&S) for approval. DoD Components will provide all requests for waiver or exception, including those approved by the USD(P), to the USD(I&S) through the Director, Security Policy and Oversight Division. The USD(I&S) and USD(P) shall be responsible for promptly notifying the Director, ISOO, of approved waivers and exceptions involving References (d) and (f).

d. Requests for information security waivers and exceptions shall contain sufficient information to permit a complete and thorough analysis to be made of the impact of approval on national security. Minimally, requests must identify the specific provision(s) of this Manual for which the waiver or exception is sought (cite this Manual by volume, enclosure, and paragraph) and provide rationale and justification for the request, including negative impacts to cost, schedule, mission, or operations; a mission analysis summary to identify vulnerabilities and risk management considerations; a summary of proposed mitigation measures to reduce risk; and the necessary duration for any waivers). A sample template memorandum for requesting waivers and exceptions is at the Appendix to this enclosure. Current waivers and exceptions will continue to be valid until they are due for renewal.

e. In the case of information security waivers and exceptions involving classified information, the DoD Components shall maintain documents regarding approved waivers and exceptions, and furnish such documents to other agencies with which they share affected classified information or secure facilities, except documentation regarding approved waivers and exceptions involving marking of classified information need be shared only upon request.

18. CORRECTIVE ACTIONS AND SANCTIONS

a. Procedures. Heads of the DoD Components shall establish procedures to ensure that prompt and appropriate management action is taken in cases of compromise of classified information and unauthorized disclosure of CUI, improper classification or designation of information, violation of the provisions of this Manual, and incidents that may put classified information and CUI at risk of unauthorized disclosure. Such actions shall focus on correcting or eliminating the conditions that caused or brought about the incident.

b. Sanctions

(1) DoD military and civilian personnel may be subject to criminal or administrative sanctions if they knowingly, willfully, or negligently:

(a) Disclose classified information to unauthorized persons.

(b) Classify or continue the classification of information in violation of this Volume.

(c) Create or continue a SAP contrary to the requirements of Reference (q) and this Volume.

(d) Disclose CUI to unauthorized persons.

(e) Violate any other provision of this Manual.

(2) Sanctions include, but are not limited to, warning, reprimand, suspension without pay, forfeiture of pay, removal, discharge, loss, or denial of access to classified information and/or CUI, and removal of classification authority. Criminal sanctions may also be undertaken in accordance with sections 801-940 of title 10, U.S.C. (also known as "The Uniform Code of Military Justice" (UCMJ) (Reference (ax)) and other applicable U.S. criminal laws.

(3) If an individual delegated OCA demonstrates reckless disregard or a pattern of error in applying the classification standards of this Volume, the appropriate official shall, as a minimum, remove the offending individual's OCA.

c. Reporting of Incidents. Security incidents involving classified information shall be reported as required in Enclosure 6 of Volume 3 of this Manual. Incidents involving CUI shall be reported as Volume 4 requires.

APPENDIX TO ENCLOSURE 3

DOD COMPONENT REQUEST FOR WAIVER OR EXCEPTION

[CLASSIFICATION]

COMPONENT SENIOR AGENCY OFFICIAL LETTERHEAD

[month, day, year]

MEMORANDUM FOR DIRECTOR, SECURITY POLICY AND OVERSIGHT DIVISION, OFFICE OF THE UNDER SECRETARY OF DEFENSE FOR INTELLIGENCE AND SECURITY

SUBJECT: Request for [Organization Name] Waiver [or Exception] (Information Security) from DoDM 5200.01 Standard [or Requirement]

Purpose: The [Title, Organization Name] requests a waiver or exception from DoDM 5200.01, [volume, enclosure, paragraph/section], for a [short description of the requirement or standard for which the waiver or exception is sought]. [SAO title, Organization, Name] has reviewed this request with attachments and concurs with this request.

Justification: [Brief description of the rationale and justification for the request for waiver or exception, to include negative impacts to cost, schedule, mission, or operations.]

Mission Analysis Summary: A mission analysis that discusses missions and functions impacted by this waiver or exception is at TAB A.

Risk Assessment: The risk management assessment at TAB B identifies vulnerabilities and risk management considerations related to this request for waiver or exception.

Mitigation Measures: The mitigation measures at TAB C describe measures identified to reduce risks identified at TAB B. [If there are no mitigation measures, state "None."] The [SAO Title, Organization Title] concurs with this request and the mitigation measures and accepts the risk level based on the mitigation measures to be taken.

Timeframe: This is a temporary waiver request from [start date] through [end date]. or This is a permanent exception request.

The POC for this action is [Name, Title, Organization, Phone number, email address].

[Signature Block of Component SAO]

Attachments:
As stated

[CLASSIFICATION]

ENCLOSURE 4

CLASSIFYING INFORMATION

1. TENTATIVE CLASSIFICATION. Individuals who submit information to OCAs for original classification decisions shall provide the OCA the information required by paragraphs 6.a. through 6.f. of this enclosure, and may, as necessary, tentatively classify information or documents as working papers, pending approval by the OCA. Final classification decisions must be made as soon as possible, but not later than 180 days from the initial drafting date of the document. Prior to the OCA's classification decision, such information shall be safeguarded as required for the specified level of classification and it shall not be used as a source for derivative classification.

2. DERIVATIVE CLASSIFICATION

a. When incorporating, paraphrasing, restating, or generating classified information in a new form or document (i.e., derivatively classifying information), it must be identified as classified information by marking or similar means. Derivative classification includes classification of information based on classification guidance in a security classification guide or other source material, but does not include photocopying or otherwise mechanically or electronically reproducing classified material.

b. Within the DoD all cleared personnel, who generate or create material that is to be derivatively classified, shall ensure that the derivative classification is accomplished in accordance with this enclosure. No specific, individual delegation of authority is required. DoD officials who sign or approve derivatively classified documents have principal responsibility for the quality of the derivative classification.

c. All persons performing derivative classification shall receive training, as specified in Enclosure 5 of Volume 3 of this Manual, on proper procedures for making classification determinations and properly marking derivatively classified documents.

3. RESPONSIBILITIES OF DERIVATIVE CLASSIFIERS. Derivative classifiers shall:

a. Observe and respect the classification determinations made by OCAs. If derivative classifiers believe information to be improperly classified, they shall take the actions required by section 22 of this enclosure.

b. Identify themselves and the classified information by marking it in accordance with Volume 2 of this Manual.

c. Use only authorized sources for classification guidance (e.g., security classification guides, memorandums, DoD publications, and other forms of classification guidance issued by the OCA) and markings on source documents from which the information is extracted for guidance on classification of the information in question. The use of memory alone or "general rules" about the classification of broad classes of information is prohibited.

d. Use caution when paraphrasing or restating information extracted from a classified source document. Paraphrasing or restating information may change the need for or level of classification.

e. Take appropriate and reasonable steps, including consulting a security classification guide or requesting assistance from the appropriate OCA, to resolve doubts or apparent conflicts about the classification, level of classification, and duration of classification. In cases of apparent conflict between a security classification guide and a classified source document regarding a discrete item of information, the instructions in the security classification guide shall take precedence. Where required markings are missing or omitted from source documents, consult the OCA, appropriate security classification guide, or other classification guidance for application of the omitted markings.

4. PROCEDURES FOR DERIVATIVE CLASSIFICATION

a. Derivative classifiers shall carefully analyze the material they are classifying to determine what information it contains or reveals and shall evaluate that information against the instructions provided by the classification guidance or the markings on source documents.

b. Drafters of derivatively classified documents shall portion-mark their drafts and keep records of the sources they use, to facilitate derivative classification of the finished product.

c. When material is derivatively classified based on "multiple sources" (i.e., more than one security classification guide, classified source document, or combination thereof), the derivative classifier shall compile a list of the sources used. This list shall be included in or attached to the document.

d. Duration of classification for derivatively classified documents shall be determined in accordance with section 13 of this enclosure and applied in accordance with Volume 2 of this Manual. The instructions shall not be automatically copied from source documents without consideration of adjustments that may be required (e.g., due to use of multiple sources, changes in policy, changes in classification guidance).

e. If extracting information from a document or section of a document classified by compilation, the derivative classifier shall consult the explanation on the source document to determine the appropriate classification. If that does not provide sufficient guidance, the derivative classifier shall contact the originator of the source document for assistance.

f. Infrequently, different sources of classification guidance may specify different classification for the same information. When such inconsistencies are encountered, the derivative classifier must contact the applicable OCA(s) for resolution of the inconsistency.

Pending determination, the document or material containing the information shall be protected at the highest level of classification specified by the sources.

5. DURATION OF CLASSIFICATION. Every time a classified document is created, a determination must be made regarding how long the information is to be protected (i.e., when the information will lose its sensitivity and no longer merit or qualify for classification). This is an essential part of the classification process. For derivatively classified information, the most restrictive declassification instruction (i.e., the one that specifies the longest duration of classification) must be carried forward from the source document(s), security classification guide(s) or other classification guidance provided by the OCA. Specific guidance on determining the most restrictive instruction is provided in Enclosure 3 of Volume 2.

6. CLASSIFICATION OF ACQUISITION INFORMATION. Classifying information involved in the DoD acquisition process shall conform to the requirements of DoDD 5000.01 (Reference (az)) and DoDI 5000.02 (Reference (ba)), as well as this enclosure. Security classification guides should be updated to include classified critical program information identified as part of the program protection planning process required by DoDI 5200.39 (Reference (bb)).

7. CLASSIFICATION OF INFORMATION RELEASED TO THE PUBLIC

a. Classified Information Released Without Proper Authority

(1) Classified information that has been released to the public without proper authority (e.g., media leak, data spill) remains classified. It may be declassified upon such a determination by the appropriate OCA. Enclosure 6 of Volume 3 of this Manual identifies issues to be considered when making the decision. When the determination is made that the information will remain classified, the appropriate OCA will notify known authorized holders accordingly and provide the following marking guidance to be used in the event the information is not marked:

(a) Overall level of classification.

(b) Portion markings.

(c) Identity, by name or personal identifier and position, of the OCA.

(d) Declassification instructions.

(e) Concise reason for classification.

(f) Date the action was taken.

(2) Holders of the information shall take administrative action, as needed, to apply markings and controls. DoD personnel shall not publicly acknowledge the release of classified

information and must be careful not to make any statement or comment that confirms the accuracy of or verifies the information requiring protection.

b. Reclassification of Information Declassified and Released to the Public Under Proper Authority

(1) Information that has been declassified and released to the public under proper authority may be reclassified only when:

(a) The information may be reasonably recoverable without bringing undue attention to the information, which means that:

1. Most individual recipients or holders are known and can be contacted and all forms of the information to be reclassified can be retrieved from them.

2. If the information has been made available to the public via means such as U.S. Government archives or reading rooms, it can be or has been withdrawn from public access without significant media or public attention or notice.

(b) The Secretary of Defense approves the reclassification based on a document-by-document determination and recommendation by the Head of the originating DoD Component, other than the Secretary of a Military Department, when that reclassification of the information is required to prevent significant and demonstrable damage to the national security. Reclassification and release of information under proper authority means the DoD Component with jurisdiction over the information authorized declassification and release of the information. The Secretaries of a Military Department shall approve the reclassification of information under their jurisdiction on the same basis and shall notify the USD(I&S) of the action. The Military Departments shall provide implementing guidance to their subordinate activities for submitting such requests.

(2) DoD Component Heads other than the Secretaries of the Military Departments shall submit recommendations for reclassification of information under their jurisdiction to the Secretary of Defense through the USD(I&S). Recommendations for reclassification must include, on a document-by-document basis:

(a) A description of the information.

(b) All information necessary for the original classification decision in accordance with Reference (bm), including classification level of the information and declassification instructions to be applied.

(c) When and how it was released to the public.

(d) An explanation as to why it should be reclassified. Include the applicable reason in accordance with Reference (d) and describe what damage could occur to national security. Also describe what damage may have already occurred as a result of the release.

(e) The number of recipients and/or holders and how they will be notified of the reclassification.

(f) How the information will be recovered.

(g) Whether the information is in the custody of NARA and whether the Archivist of the United States must be notified of the reclassification as specified in subparagraph 7.b.(4) of this section.

(3) Once a reclassification action has occurred, it must be reported to all recipients and holders, to the Assistant to the President for National Security Affairs (herein after referred to as "the National Security Advisor") and to ISOO within 30 days. The notification to ISOO must include how the "reasonably recoverable" decision was made, including the number of recipients or holders, how the information was recovered, and how the recipients and holders were notified. The Secretaries of the Military Departments shall notify the National Security Advisor and ISOO directly and provide an information copy to the USD(I&S). The Secretary of Defense, after making reclassification decisions, will notify the National Security Advisor and ISOO of such decisions.

(4) For documents in the physical and legal custody of NARA that have been available for public use, reclassification must also be reported to the Archivist of the United States, who shall suspend public access pending approval of the reclassification action by the Director, ISOO. The Secretaries of the Military Departments shall notify the Archivist directly and provide an information copy to USD(I&S). The Secretary of Defense will notify the Archivist as required for decisions involving other DoD Components. Disapproval of the reclassification action by the Director, ISOO, may be appealed to the President through the National Security Advisor. Public access shall remain suspended pending decision on the appeal.

(a) OCAs shall notify the Secretary of Defense of the need to appeal ISOO decisions through their DoD Component Head and the USD(I&S).

(b) Notifications shall clearly articulate the compelling national security reasons for reclassifying the information and shall counter the ISOO rationale for disapproving the reclassification.

(5) Once a final decision is rendered, OCAs shall update their security classification guidance accordingly. The reclassified information must be marked and safeguarded in accordance with the requirements of Volumes 2 and 3 of this Manual.

(6) Any cleared recipients or holders of reclassified information shall be notified and appropriately briefed about their continuing legal obligations and responsibilities to protect this information from unauthorized disclosure. The recipients or holder who do not have security clearances shall, to the extent practicable, be appropriately briefed about the reclassification of the information to which they have had access and their obligation not to disclose the information, and shall be asked to sign an acknowledgement of the briefing and to return all copies of the information in their possession.

c. Information Declassified and Released to the Public Without Proper Authority. Information that was declassified without proper authority remains classified. See paragraph 7.a. of this enclosure and paragraph 1.c. of Enclosure 5 of this Volume.

8. CLASSIFICATION OR RECLASSIFICATION FOLLOWING RECEIPT OF A REQUEST FOR INFORMATION. Information that has not previously been released to the public under proper authority may be classified or reclassified after receiving a request for it under FOIA; section 2204(c)(1) of Reference (av) (also known as "The Presidential Records Act of 1978"); section 552a of Reference (ay) (also known and hereinafter referred to as "The Privacy Act of 1974, as amended"); or the mandatory review provisions of section 3.5 of Reference (d), only if it is done on a document-by-document basis with the personal participation or under the direction of the USD(I&S), the Secretary or Under Secretary of a Military Department, or the senior agency official appointed within a Military Department in accordance with section 5.4(d) of Reference (d). OCAs shall submit requests to the USD(I&S) through the Head of the DoD Component.

a. The provisions of this section apply to information that has been declassified in accordance with the date or event specified by the OCA as well as to information not previously classified.

b. Classification requests shall provide all information necessary for the original classification process as specified by Reference (bm).

c. The Secretaries of the Military Departments shall notify the USD(I&S) of classification decisions made in accordance with the provisions of this section.

d. Once a decision is rendered, OCAs shall update their security classification guidance as needed.

9. CLASSIFYING NON-GOVERNMENT RESEARCH AND DEVELOPMENT INFORMATION

a. Information that is a product of contractor or individual independent research and development (IR&D) or bid and proposal (B&P) efforts, as defined by DoDI 3204.01 (Reference (bc)), conducted without prior or current access to classified information associated with the specific information in question, may not be classified unless:

(1) The U.S. Government first acquires a proprietary interest in the information; or,

(2) The contractor or individual conducting the IR&D or B&P requests that the U.S. Government contracting activity place the information under the control of the security classification system without relinquishing ownership of the information.

b. The contractor or individual conducting such an IR&D or B&P effort and believing that the information generated may require protection in the interest of national security shall safeguard the information and submit it to an appropriate U.S. Government activity for a classification determination.

(1) The U.S. Government activity receiving the request shall issue security classification guidance, as appropriate, if the information is to be classified. If the information is not under the activity's classification authority, the activity shall refer the matter to the appropriate classification authority and inform the individual or contractor of the referral. The information shall be safeguarded until the matter is resolved.

(2) The U.S. Government activity authorizing classification for the information shall verify whether the contractor or individual is cleared and has been authorized to store classified information. If not, the U.S. Government activity authorizing classification shall advise whether security clearance action should be initiated.

(3) If the contractor or individual refuses to be processed for the appropriate security clearance and the U.S. Government does not acquire a proprietary interest in the information, the information may not be classified.

(4) If the information is not classified, consideration may be given to the need for other controls applicable to unclassified information (e.g., export controls). (See Volume 4 of this Manual for guidance on CUI.)

10. THE PATENT SECRECY ACT OF 1952. Sections 181 through 188 of title 35, U.S.C. (also known and hereinafter referred to as "The Patent Secrecy Act of 1952" (Reference (bd)) provides that the Secretary of Defense, among others, may determine that disclosure of an invention by granting of a patent would be detrimental to the national security. The Department of Defense shall handle a patent application on which a secrecy order has been imposed as follows:

a. If the patent application contains information that warrants classification, it shall be assigned a classification and be marked and safeguarded commensurate with the level of classification.

b. Unclassified patent applications that do not contain information that warrants classification, but requires CUI safeguarding and dissemination controls, will be marked as a category of CUI in accordance with Volume 4 of this Manual. This same requirement applies to legacy patent applications marked with the former statement that required handling as CONFIDENTIAL.

11. REQUESTS FOR CLASSIFICATION DETERMINATION. Within 30 days of receipt OCAs shall provide a classification determination to requests for same from individuals who are not OCAs, but who believe they have originated information requiring classification. If the

information is not under the OCA's classification authority, the request shall be referred to the appropriate OCA and the requestor shall be informed of the referral. Pending a classification determination the information shall be protected consistent with the requirements of this Manual.

12. CHALLENGES TO CLASSIFICATION

a. Principles. If holders of information have substantial reason to believe that the information is improperly or unnecessarily classified, they shall communicate that belief to their security manager or the OCA to bring about any necessary correction. This may be done informally or by submitting a formal challenge to the classification in accordance with References (d) and (f).

(1) Informal questioning of classification is encouraged before resorting to formal challenge. If the information holder has reason to believe the classification applied to information is inappropriate, he or she should contact the classifier of the source document or material to resolve the issue.

(2) The Heads of the DoD Components shall ensure that no retribution is taken against any individual for questioning a classification or making a formal challenge to a classification.

(3) Formal challenges to classification made pursuant to this section shall include sufficient description of the information being challenged to permit identification of the information and its classifier with reasonable effort. Challenges to classification made by DoD personnel shall also include the reason why the challenger believes that the information is improperly or unnecessarily classified. The challenge shall be unclassified, if possible.

(4) Pending final decision on the classification level, the information that is the subject of a classification challenge will remain classified at its current classification level or the recommended change level, whichever is higher. The information will continue to be safeguarded unless and until a decision is made to declassify it.

(5) The provisions of this section do not apply to information required to be submitted for prepublication review or other administrative process pursuant to an approved NDA.

b. Procedures. The Heads of the DoD Components shall encourage classification challenges and establish procedures for handling challenges to classification received from within and from outside their Components in accordance with Reference (f). The DoD Components shall:

(1) Incorporate the following language for Component security classification guides consistent with the intent of Section 5.3 of Reference (d):

(a) Follow the guidance provided in Paragraph 12 of this enclosure for individuals who wish to challenge information they believe has been improperly or unnecessarily classified.

(b) Such challenges are encouraged, and expected, and should be forwarded through the appropriate channels to the office of primary responsibility.

(c) Pending final decision, handle and protect the information at its current classification level or at the recommended change level, whichever is higher.

(d) Challenges should include sufficient description to permit identification of the specific information under challenge with reasonable effort.

(e) Challenges should include detailed justification outlining why the information is improperly or unnecessarily classified.

(2) Establish a system for processing, tracking, and recording formal challenges to classification, including administrative appeals of classification decisions, and ensure that DoD Component personnel are made aware of the established procedures for classification challenges.

(3) Provide an opportunity for review of the information by an impartial official or panel.

(4) Except as provided in subparagraphs 12.b.(5) and (6) of this section, provide an initial written response to each challenge within 60 days. If not responding fully to the challenge within 60 days, the DoD Component shall acknowledge the challenge and provide an expected date of response. This acknowledgment shall include a statement that, if no response is received within 120 days, the challenger has the right to forward the challenge to the ISCAP for decision. The challenger may also forward the challenge to the ISCAP if the Component has not responded to an appeal within 90 days of receipt of the appeal. DoD Component responses to those challenges it denies shall include the challenger's right to appeal to the ISCAP.

(5) Not process the challenge if it concerns information that has been the subject of a challenge within the preceding 2 years or is the subject of pending litigation. The DoD Component shall inform the challenger of the situation and appropriate appellate procedures.

(6) Refer challenges involving RD to the Department of the Energy and FRD to the Deputy Assistant Secretary of Defense, Nuclear Matters (DASD(NM)) and notify the challenger accordingly. Do not include a statement about forwarding the challenge to the ISCAP in the notification letter, as these categories of information are not within the purview of the ISCAP.

(7) In case a classification challenge involves documents that contain RD and/or FRD as well as information classified under Reference (d), delete (redact) the RD and FRD portions of the documents before the document is forwarded to the ISCAP for review.

ENCLOSURE 5

DECLASSIFICATION AND CHANGES IN CLASSIFICATION

1. DECLASSIFICATION POLICY

a. Per Reference (d), information shall be declassified as soon as it no longer meets the standards for classification. In some exceptional cases, the need to protect information still meeting these standards may be outweighed by the public interest in disclosure of the information, and in these cases the information should be declassified. Pursuant to DoD policy in Reference (b), information shall remain classified only as long as:

(1) It is in the best interest of national security to keep it protected.

(2) Continued classification is in accordance with the requirements of Reference (d).

b. If DoD officials have reason to believe that the public interest in disclosure of information outweighs the need for continued classification, they shall refer the matter to the appropriate senior agency official appointed in accordance with section 5.4(d) of Reference (d), who shall consult with the OCA. The senior agency official shall determine whether to declassify the information.

c. Classified information that has been declassified without proper authority remains classified until declassified by an OCA with jurisdiction over the information.

(1) Administrative action shall be taken to restore markings and controls, as appropriate.

(2) If the information is in records in the physical and legal custody of NARA and has been made available to the public:

(a) The OCA shall, as part of determining if restoration of markings and controls is appropriate, consider whether removing the information from public access will significantly mitigate harm to the national security or otherwise draw undue attention to the information.

(b) DoD or Military Department senior agency official shall provided written notification to the Archivist of the United States, which shall include a description of the record(s), the elements of information that are classified, the duration of classification, and the specific authority for continued classification. OCAs in DoD Components other than the Military Departments shall submit notifications to USD(I&S), through their chain of command, for submission to the Archivist.

(c) The issue shall be referred to the Director, ISOO if the information is more than 25 years old and the Archivist does not agree with the OCA's determination that the information remains classified. The information shall be withdrawn from public access pending resolution.

d. Classified information shall be marked as declassified, as specified by Enclosure 3 of Volume 2 of this Manual, before it is handled as unclassified. Holders of classified information marked with a date or event on the "declassify on" line shall, when the date or event has passed, confirm that the OCA(s) of the information has not extended the classification period. This can be done by reference to a security classification or declassification guide or to other appropriate guidance issued by the OCA or by consultation with the OCA. Once declassification is confirmed, such information may be made publicly available only as provided in paragraph 1.e of this section.

e. Declassification does not authorize release of the information to the public. DECLASSIFIED INFORMATION SHALL NOT BE RELEASED TO THE PUBLIC UNTIL A PUBLIC RELEASE REVIEW AS REQUIRED BY REFERENCES (V) AND (W) HAS BEEN CONDUCTED to determine if there are reasons for withholding some or all of the information. Declassified information may be released to the public unless withholding is appropriate in accordance with other applicable law (for example, FOIA or the Privacy Act of 1974, as amended) or DoD issuance (for example, Reference (v) and DoDD 5230.25 (Reference (be)). Regardless of the date specified for declassification, declassified information shall not be approved for public release without referral to the OCA of the information, except records accessioned by NARA that were reviewed for automatic declassification in accordance with section 3.3 of Reference (d) will be reviewed by NARA for public release.

f. Personnel leaving DoD employment or service may not direct that information be declassified in order to remove it from DoD control.

g. OCAs affected by ISCAP deliberations shall be notified of the final decision and shall consider the need to change classification and declassification guides to reflect the specific ISCAP decision.

2. <u>PROCESSES FOR DECLASSIFICATION</u>. Reference (d) establishes four separate and parallel processes for declassifying information:

a. A process requiring the original classifier to decide at the time information is classified when it may be declassified.

b. A process that shall cause information of permanent historical value to be automatically declassified no later than 31 December of the year that is 25 years from the date of its origin unless specific action is taken to keep it classified.

c. A process for reviewing information for possible declassification upon request (mandatory declassification review).

d. A process for systematic review of information for possible declassification.

3. AUTHORITY TO DECLASSIFY

a. Information may be declassified or downgraded by the cognizant OCA, by supervisory officials of the OCA if the supervisory official has OCA, or by those officials who have been delegated declassification authority in accordance with paragraph 3.b. of this enclosure. The authority to declassify information extends only to information for which the specific official has classification, program, or functional responsibility.

b. DoD Component Heads with OCA may designate officials within their organizations to exercise declassification authority (e.g., make declassification decisions, issue declassification guidance) over specific types or categories of information for which they are responsible. Delegations of declassification authority shall be reported concurrently to the Director of Security, OUSD(I&S). Other OCAs may designate members of their staffs to exercise declassification authority over information under their jurisdiction. Declassification authorities, other than original classifiers, shall receive training as specified in section 6 of Enclosure 5, Volume 3 of this Manual upon initial designation and every 2 years thereafter.

c. Pursuant to section 7 of this enclosure, only NSA/CSS is authorized to downgrade or declassify cryptologic information.

d. If the activity originating the classified information no longer exists, the activity that inherited the functions of the originating activity shall determine what constitutes appropriate declassification action. If the functions of the originating activity were dispersed to more than one activity, the inheriting activity(ies) cannot be determined, or the functions have ceased to exist, the senior agency official of the DoD Component of the originating activity shall determine the declassification action to be taken.

e. Information originated by another agency or DoD Component shall be referred to the originator for downgrading or declassification determinations.

f. Declassification of information is an inherently governmental function that must be performed by a properly trained and authorized U.S. Government employee having the explicit permission of the government organization that originated the information. DoD Components must organize for and provide adequate resources to execute this mission while protecting the national security. Contractors may perform routine administrative, pre-processing, and technology support functions, as well as make recommendations for declassification of information. U.S. Government personnel must sample contractors' declassification recommendations at a rate of no less than 5 percent of the total volume of records being processed for declassification, before making the formal decision to declassify the information.

4. DECLASSIFICATION GUIDANCE. Persons with declassification authority shall develop and issue declassification guidance to facilitate effective review and declassification of information classified under both current and previous classified national security information Executive orders. The guidance may be in the form of declassification guides, sections of

security classification guides, memorandums, etc. Exemptions authorized in accordance with section 13 of this enclosure should be cited in declassification guidance.

5. DECLASSIFICATION OF INFORMATION

a. Holders of classified information marked with a date or event on the "declassify on" line, shall, prior to downgrading or declassifying the information, confirm that the OCA(s) for the information has not extended the classification period.

b. Holders of classified information may confirm the classification period (i.e., date or event for declassification) by reference to the applicable security classification or declassification guide or other appropriate guidance issued by the OCA(s), or by consultation with the OCA(s). Classified information shall continue to be safeguarded as required for the indicated classification level until the holder has confirmed that the OCA(s) has not extended the classification period.

c. If the holder of a document has reason to believe it should not be declassified as specified, the originator shall be notified through appropriate administrative channels. The document or material shall continue to be protected at the originally assigned classification until the issue is resolved.

d. Declassification markings are used to clearly convey the declassified status of the information and who authorized the declassification. All declassified information in agency records not held by NARA shall have the declassification markings required by Enclosure 3 of Volume 2 of this Manual applied.

6. CANCELING OR CHANGING CLASSIFICATION MARKINGS. Declassification authority is not required for simply canceling or changing classification markings in accordance with guidance from an OCA or declassification authority. Sections 18 and 19 of this enclosure provide guidance on downgrading and upgrading classified information.

7. SPECIAL PROCEDURES FOR CRYPTOLOGIC INFORMATION. Only NSA/CSS may declassify cryptologic information. Therefore, such information uncovered in systematic or mandatory review of U.S. Government records for declassification, including such information incorporated into other documents, must be referred to the NSA/CSS for declassification determination.

a. Recognition of cryptologic information is not always easy since it may concern or reveal the processes, techniques, operations, and scope of signals intelligence, which consists of communications intelligence, electronic intelligence, and foreign instrumentation signals intelligence, or it may concern IA, which includes COMSEC, including the communications portion of cover and deception plans. Much cryptologic information is also considered FGI.

b. NSA/CSS has established special procedures for mandatory review for declassification of classified cryptologic information. For questions regarding cryptographic equities or for referrals for declassification determination, contact:

Director, National Security Agency/
Chief, Central Security Service
ATTN: Declassification Services (DJP5)
Fort George G. Meade, MD 20755-6248

8. PERMANENTLY VALUABLE RECORDS

a. Classified information in records that are scheduled for retention by NARA as permanently valuable records when that information is less than 20 years old shall be subject to the automatic declassification provisions of section 12 of this enclosure when the information is 25 years old.

b. Classified information in records that are scheduled for retention by NARA as permanently valuable records when that information is already more than 20 years old shall be subject to the automatic declassification provisions of section 12 of this enclosure 5 years from the date the records are scheduled.

9. RECORDS DETERMINED NOT TO HAVE PERMANENT HISTORICAL VALUE. Classified records determined not to be permanently valuable and not scheduled retention by NARA are subject to the automatic declassification provisions of this issuance. The disposition (destruction) date of those records in the DoD Component's Records Control Schedule or General Records Schedule approved by NARA shall be used as the declassification date, although the duration of classification may be extended if a record has been retained for business reasons beyond its scheduled destruction date. If the disposition date extends beyond 25 years, an exemption request must be submitted to and approved by the ISCAP in accordance with the procedure in section 13 of this enclosure.

10. EXTENDING CLASSIFICATION BEYOND 25 YEARS FOR UNSCHEDULED RECORDS. For unscheduled classified records (both permanent and temporary), the duration of classification beyond 25 years shall be determined when the records are scheduled (i.e., when NARA has approved a records control schedule that can be used to determine their final disposition). Permanently valuable records must be scheduled before they are 25 years old in order to request ISCAP approval to extend classification beyond 25 years when applicable. Contact the DoD Component Records Manager for further guidance on scheduling records.

11. CLASSIFIED INFORMATION IN THE CUSTODY OF CONTRACTORS, LICENSEES, GRANTEES, OR OTHER AUTHORIZED PRIVATE ORGANIZATIONS OR INDIVIDUALS. Pursuant to the provisions of Reference (ab), DoD Components must provide security

classification and declassification guidance to contractors, licensees, grantees, or other authorized private organizations or individuals who possess DoD classified information. DoD Components must also determine if classified records are held by such entities, and, if so, whether they are permanent records of historical value and thus subject to automatic declassification. Until such a determination has been made by an appropriate official, the classified information contained in such records shall not be subject to automatic declassification and shall be safeguarded in accordance with the most recent security classification or declassification guidance provided by the DoD Component.

12. AUTOMATIC DECLASSIFICATION. Reference (d) establishes a system for declassification of information in permanently valuable historical records. DoD Component declassification activities shall conduct reviews of records eligible for automatic declassification in accordance with the procedures specified in this enclosure and Reference (f) and by the NDC.

a. Deadline. All permanently valuable records shall be reviewed for declassification by December 31 of the year in which they become 25 years old. Unless the document warrants continued classification in accordance with an authorized exclusion (see paragraph 12.e of this section) or an ISCAP-approved exemption (see section 13 of this enclosure), or qualifies for a delay of automatic declassification in accordance with paragraph 12.g. of this section, the documents shall be declassified.

(1) Documents not reviewed by December 31 of the year in which they become 25 years old shall be automatically declassified unless the onset of automatic declassification has been delayed in accordance with paragraph 12.g. of this section or an exemption has been approved.

(2) Documents exempted from declassification shall be automatically declassified on December 31 of the year in which they become 50 years old or, as appropriate, 75 years old unless further exempted from declassification in accordance with section 13 of this enclosure.

(3) If the document's date of origin cannot be readily determined, the date of original classification shall be used to determine the automatic declassification deadline.

b. Secretary of Defense Certification. In addition to the requirement of paragraph 12.a. of this section, DoD Components shall not automatically declassify DoD records without reviewing them for declassification unless the Secretary of Defense has certified to Congress that such declassification would not harm the national security pursuant to section 1041(c) of Public Law 106-65 (Reference (bf)). If records will not be reviewed for declassification as required prior to December 31 of the year in which they become 25 years old, the DoD Component Heads shall notify the USD(I&S), 6 months in advance of the deadline, so the required Secretary of Defense certification can be addressed. Notification shall include identification of the records, the compelling reason why the records will not be reviewed by the deadline, how many records will remain un-reviewed, where the records are located, and when the required reviews will be completed.

c. Public Release of Automatically Declassified Documents. Automatic declassification does not constitute approval for public release of the information. Automatically declassified documents shall not be released to the public until a public disclosure review has been conducted in accordance with paragraph 1.e. of this enclosure. Declassified information may be designated CUI in accordance with Volume 4 of this Manual if it meets the criteria for designation; information so designated shall be marked and protected as Volume 4 requires.

d. Basis for Exclusion or Exemption from Automatic Declassification. Information shall be excluded or exempted from automatic declassification provisions based on content. Exclusion or exemption shall not be based solely on the type of document or record in which the information is found.

e. Exclusion of RD and FRD. Documents and other materials marked or containing RD or FRD are excluded from the automatic declassification provisions of Reference (d) and this Volume until the RD or FRD designation is properly removed. Such information shall remain classified or shall be referred for a declassification review to the Department of Energy if RD or the DASD(NM) if FRD.

(1) In accordance with the provisions of section 3161 of Public Law 105-261 (Reference (bg) (also known as "The Kyl-Lott Amendment"), and its implementing plan, all personnel who perform automatic declassification reviews on records that are highly likely to contain RD or FRD must be trained and certified by the Department of Energy in the identification of unmarked RD and FRD information. DoD Components shall report each confirmed inadvertent release of RD or FRD occurring during declassification processes to the Department of Energy and provide a copy to OUSD(I&S) Security Directorate.

(2) When the RD or FRD pertains to defense nuclear information, declassification reviews shall be referred to the DASD(NM), who has OCA for defense nuclear information, to include joint OCA with the Department of Energy for FRD.

(3) The Secretary of Energy determines when information concerning foreign nuclear programs that was removed from the RD category in order to carry out provisions of section 2673 of Reference (af) may be declassified. Unless otherwise determined by the appropriate OCA, such information shall be declassified when comparable information concerning the U.S. nuclear program is declassified.

f. Integral File Block. Classified records within an integral file block that are otherwise subject to automatic declassification in accordance with this section shall not be automatically declassified until December 31 of the year that is 25 years from the date of the MOST RECENT record or the date specified by the exemption instruction of the most recent exempted record, whichever is later, within the file block. For purposes of automatic declassification, integral file blocks shall contain only records dated within 10 years of the oldest record in the file block.

g. Delays of Automatic Declassification. The following lists the scenarios for which automatic declassification may be delayed.

(1) Media That Is Difficult or Costly to Review. Before the records are subject to automatic declassification, a DoD Component Head or senior agency official may delay automatic declassification for up to 5 additional years for classified information contained in media that make a review for possible declassification more difficult or costly. Prior to taking such action, officials shall consult with the NDC Director, either through the Component declassification plan or by memorandum. The Heads of the Military Departments or their senior agency official shall consult with the NDC Director directly and provide an information copy to the Deputy Under Secretary of Defense Intelligence and Security (DUSD(I&S)). Other DoD Component Heads or their senior agency official shall consult with the NDC Director through DUSD(I&S).

(a) When determined by NARA or jointly determined by NARA and the Department of Defense, automatic declassification may be delayed for:

1. Records requiring extraordinary preservation or conservation treatment, to include reformatting, to preclude damage to the records by declassification processing.

2. Records that pose a potential menace to health, life, or property due to contamination by a hazardous substance.

3. Electronic media if the media is subject to issues of software or hardware obsolescence or degraded data.

(b) Information contained in such media that has been referred shall be automatically declassified 5 years from the date of notification or 30 years from the date of origination of the media, whichever is longer, unless the information has been properly exempted.

(2) Newly Discovered Records. The Director, ISOO, must be consulted whenever a DoD Component Head determines there is a need to delay automatic declassification for newly discovered records that were inadvertently not reviewed prior to the effective date of automatic declassification. Such consultation shall occur not later than 90 days from discovery of the records. Heads of the Military Departments or their senior agency official will notify ISOO directly and provide an information copy to DUSD(I&S). Other DoD Component Heads or their senior agency official will notify ISOO through the DUSD(I&S). The notification should identify the records and their volume, explain the circumstances leading to discovery of the missed records, and provide the anticipated date for declassification. A DoD Component has up to 3 years from the date of discovery to make a declassification, exemption, or referral determination. Referral to other DoD Components or Federal entities with identified interests or equities shall be in accordance with subparagraph 12.g.(3) and section 15 of this enclosure.

(3) Referred Records

(a) Referring Other Agency Information. Other than records that are properly excluded or exempted from automatic declassification, records containing classified information originated by another department or agency or the disclosure of which would affect the interests or activities of other departments or agencies with respect to the classified information and that could reasonably be expected to fall under one or more of the exemptions identified in paragraph 13.b. of this enclosure shall be identified prior to onset of automatic declassification for later referral to those departments or agencies. DoD Components shall identify other agency information for referral during the initial review of Component records; referral review will take place under the auspices of the NDC. The records shall be referred using SF 715, "U.S. Government Declassification Review Tab."

(b) Referrals to the Department of Defense. Other agency records subject to automatic declassification that contain defense information shall be reviewed by the appropriate DoD Component upon referral. If a final determination is not provided within 1 year on a referral made by the NDC, defense information in the referred records shall be automatically declassified.

(c) DoD Component Referrals to Other DoD Components. Records containing information originated by another DoD Component or the disclosure of which would affect the interests or activities of another DoD Component with respect to the classified information shall be referred and processed through the NDC, as appropriate. The DoD Component shall be notified of these types of referrals.

(d) Referral Review Period. If any disagreement arises between a DoD Component and the NDC regarding the referral review period, the DoD Component shall notify ISOO and USD(I&S) of the disagreement. In such cases, the Director of ISOO shall determine the appropriate review period for referred records. Otherwise, the DoD Component shall provide a final determination on referrals received through the NDC within 1 year of referral or the information shall be automatically declassified. If any disagreement arises among the DoD Components regarding the referral review period, the USD(I&S) shall determine the appropriate period of review for the referred records.

h. Automatic Declassification of Backlogged Records at NARA. In accordance with Presidential Memorandum (Reference (bh)) and under NDC direction:

(1) Referrals and quality assurance problems within the backlog of more than 400 million pages of accessioned Federal records previously subject to automatic declassification shall be addressed in a manner that will permit public access to all declassified records from this backlog no later than December 31, 2013.

(2) DoD Components shall review all referrals to DoD in the backlogged records and identify potentially exemptible information for further referral to other agencies. For DoD, the backlog includes all records reviewed for automatic declassification from April 1995 to December 2009 that have been accessioned, but not processed, by NARA.

i. Declassification Review Technique. DoD Components may use a pass/fail or a redaction declassification technique when doing automatic declassification reviews.

13. EXEMPTIONS FROM AUTOMATIC DECLASSIFICATION. Reference (d) sets out three types of exemptions, specific criteria and duration, and the requirements for requesting an exemption from automatic declassification. Information not exempted from automatic declassification shall be automatically declassified no later than December 31 of the year that is 25 years from the date of origin. Information exempted from automatic declassification remains subject to the mandatory and systematic declassification review provisions of this Volume.

a. Exemption Types

(1) Specific Information. This exemption option permits OCAs to identify and select specific information that should be exempted from the automatic declassification provisions. The information is described topically in a manner similar to how topics of information are described in a security classification guide and must fall within one or more of the exemption categories described in paragraph 13.b. of this section.

(2) Specific Records. This exemption option permits OCAs to identify and select specific records for exemption from the automatic declassification provisions. The records must be described at the records title level and must contain information that is eligible for exemption under one or more of the exemption categories described in paragraph 13.b. of this section.

(3) File Series. This exemption option allows OCAs to identify an entire file series that should be exempted from the automatic declassification provisions. File series shall be considered for exemption only after a review or assessment has determined that the series is replete with information that almost invariably falls within one or more of the exemption categories described in paragraph 13.b. of this section.

b. Exemption Criteria and Duration

(1) Exempting 25-Year-Old Information. Information that is 25 years old may be exempted (by topic or file series) from automatic declassification for a period not to exceed 50 years from the date of origin when the release would clearly and demonstrably be expected to:

(a) Reveal the identity of a confidential human source, a human intelligence source, a relationship with an intelligence or security service of a foreign government or international organization, or a non-human intelligence source; or impair the effectiveness of an intelligence method currently in use, available for use, or under development (exemption 25X1);

(b) Reveal information that would assist in the development, production, or use of weapons of mass destruction (exemption 25X2);

(c) Reveal information that would impair U.S. cryptologic systems or activities (exemption 25X3);

(d) Reveal information that would impair the application of state-of-the-art technology within a U.S. weapon system (exemption 25X4);

(e) Reveal formally named or numbered U.S. Military war plans that remain in effect, or reveal operational or tactical elements of prior plans that are contained in such active plans (exemption 25X5);

(f) Reveal information, including FGI, that would cause serious harm to relations between the United States and a foreign government, or to ongoing diplomatic activities of the United States (exemption 25X6);

(g) Reveal information that would impair the current ability of U.S. Government officials to protect the President, Vice President, and other protectees for whom protection services, in the interest of the national security, are authorized (exemption 25X7);

(h) Reveal information that would seriously impair current national security emergency preparedness plans or reveal current vulnerabilities of systems, installations, or infrastructures relating to the national security (exemption 25X8); or

(i) Violate a statute, treaty, or international agreement that does not permit the automatic or unilateral declassification of information at 25 years (exemption 25X9).

(2) Exempting 50-Year-Old Information. Information that is 50 years old may continue to be exempted (by topic or files series) from automatic declassification for an additional 25 years (i.e., for a period not to exceed 75 years from the date of origin) when:

(a) The release would clearly and demonstrably be expected to reveal the identity of a confidential human source or a human intelligence source (exemption 50X1-HUM), or key design concepts of weapons of mass destruction (exemption 50X2-WMD), or

(b) In extraordinary cases, the Secretary of Defense or the Secretary of a Military Department, or their senior agency officials, as appropriate, proposes within 5 years of the onset of automatic declassification to further exempt specific information from declassification at 50 years. The exemption category numbers are the same as for 25 year exemptions, except the number "50" shall be used in place of "25."

(3) Exempting 75-Year-Old Information. The Secretary of Defense or the Secretaries of the Military Departments, or their senior agency officials, as appropriate, may propose within 5 years of the onset of automatic declassification to further exempt specific information from declassification at 75 years. Such proposals must be formally accepted by the ISCAP. The exemption category numbers are the same as for 25 year exemptions, except the number "75" shall be used in place of "25."

(4) File Series Exemptions Approved Prior to December 31, 2008. File series exemptions approved by the President prior to December 31, 2008, shall remain valid without any additional DoD Component action pending ISCAP review by the later of December 31, 2010, or December 31 of the year that is 10 years from the date of previous approval.

(5) Declassification of 50-Year-Old Information in Previously Exempted Records. All previously exempted records, both file series and specific information, that are 50 years or older as of December 31, 2012, shall be automatically declassified by that date unless further exempted in accordance with subparagraphs 13.b.(2) through 13.b.(4) of this section. All existing records meeting the criteria shall be processed for declassification by December 31, 2012. Declassification actions shall be accomplished in accordance with the schedule and priority issued by the NDC. After December 31, 2012, previously exempted records shall be automatically declassified on December 31 of the year that is no more than 50 years from the date of origin unless further exempted in accordance with this section.

c. Exemption Requests. Requests for exemption shall include all information necessary for making a decision. Requests to extend the duration of an exemption shall be processed in the same manner as an initial request.

(1) Requesting an Exemption for Specific Information or Specific Records. OCAs shall provide the following information:

(a) A detailed description of the information, in the form of a declassification guide.

(b) An explanation of why the information should be exempt from automatic declassification and must remain classified for a longer period of time.

(c) A specific date or a specific and independently verifiable event for automatic declassification of specific records that contain the information proposed for exemption. The date or event shall not exceed December 31 of the year that is 50 years from the date of origin of the records (75 years for 50 year old material), except a date or event is not required when the information identifies a confidential human source or a human intelligence source or key design concepts of weapons of mass destruction.

(d) If appropriate, a statement that the exemption will be cited subsequently in applicable classification guides to provide declassification guidance.

(e) If requesting an exemption from declassification at 50 or 75 years, a statement of support from the USD(I&S), as the designee of the Secretary of Defense. DoD Components that are elements of the Intelligence Community shall also provide a statement of support from the DNI.

(2) Requesting an Exemption for a File Series. OCAs shall provide the following information:

(a) A description of the file series.

(b) An explanation of why the information within the file series is almost invariably exempt from automatic declassification and why the information must remain classified for a longer period of time.

(c) A specific date or event for declassification of the information, not to exceed December 31 of the year that is 50 years from the date of origin of the records (75 years for 50 year old information), except a date or event is not required when the information within the file series almost invariably identifies a confidential human source or a human intelligence source or key design concepts of weapons of mass destruction.

(d) If appropriate, a statement that the exemption will be cited subsequently in applicable classification guides to provide declassification guidance.

(e) If requesting an exemption from declassification at 50 or 75 years, a statement of support from the USD(I&S), as the designee of Secretary of Defense. DoD Components that are elements of the Intelligence Community shall also provide a statement of support from the DNI.

d. When to Request an Exemption. Exemptions shall be requested not more than 5 years and not less than 1 year before information is subject to automatic declassification except for 75- year exemptions which shall be requested in accordance with subparagraph 13.b.(3) of this section.

e. Who Identifies and Requests an Exemption. In all cases, OCAs are responsible for identifying information that should be exempted from automatic declassification. The type of exemption requested (i.e., specific information, specific records, or file series) determines who must request the exemption.

(1) Specific Information and Specific Records. The senior agency official of a Military Department or the USD(I&S) acting as the DoD senior agency official, as appropriate, requests exemptions for specific information and specific records from automatic declassification. OCAs, except those in a Military Department, shall request exemptions for specific information and specific records through their DoD Component Head to USD(I&S). USD(I&S) shall notify the Director of ISOO, serving as Executive Secretary of the ISCAP, of any information or records that the Component proposes to exempt from automatic declassification. OCAs within a Military Department shall request exemptions through their Department's senior agency official, who shall notify the Director of ISOO and provide USD(I&S) an information copy for oversight purposes.

(2) File Series. For file series exemptions, the Secretary of Defense or the Secretary of a Military Department, as appropriate, must request the exemption. In either case, the request is forwarded to the Director of ISOO, serving as Executive Secretary of the ISCAP. OCAs, except those within a Military Department, shall submit requests for file series exemption through their DoD Component Head to USD(I&S). USD(I&S) will forward the request to the Secretary of Defense for decision and ISCAP notification. OCAs within the Military Departments shall submit requests for exemption to the Secretary of the Military Department, who shall notify the ISCAP. Military Departments shall provide USD(I&S) an information copy of such notifications for oversight purposes.

f. ISCAP Authority. The ISCAP may direct the Department of Defense not to exempt the specific information, specific records, or file series, or to declassify it at an earlier date than recommended. The Secretary of Defense or the Secretary of a Military Department, as appropriate, may appeal such a decision to the President through the National Security Advisor. The information will remain classified while such an appeal is pending. OCAs shall notify the appropriate DoD authority if an appeal is necessary and provide justification and rationale to counter the ISCAP decision. Military Departments shall provide USD(I&S) an information copy of any appeal for oversight purposes.

g. Notice to Information Holders. When information has been approved for exemption by the ISCAP, the OCA must notify all known information holders. This may be done through issuance of a memorandum or distribution of the declassification guide. DoD Components that have ISCAP-approved declassification guides must ensure maximum dissemination to record holders of the information. Holders shall re-mark documents in their possession to reflect the exemption.

14. DECLASSIFICATION OF INFORMATION MARKED WITH OLD DECLASSIFICATION INSTRUCTIONS

a. In accordance with Reference (f), when information is marked with previously authorized exemption categories X-1 through X-8, or with the instructions "OADR" (Originating Agency's Determination Required) or "MR" (Manual Review), including when preceded by "Source marked," use a declassification date of 25 years from the date of the source document or 25 years from the current date if the source document date is not available, unless exempted in accordance with section 13 of this enclosure.

b. If imagery subject to E.O. 12951 (Reference (bi)) is marked with the declassification instruction "DCI Only" or "DNI Only," use "25X1, E.O. 12951" as the declassification instruction, as specified by the DNI. (Contact the National Geospatial-Intelligence Agency, Classification Management (NGA/SISX) for assistance in determining whether specific imagery is subject to E.O. 12951.) Otherwise, for documents marked with the declassification instructions "DCI Only" or "DNI Only" which do NOT contain information subject to Reference (bi), use a declassification date that is 25 years from the date of the source document or 25 years from the current date if the source document date is not available.

15. REFERRALS IN THE AUTOMATIC DECLASSIFICATION PROCESS. Referrals are required by References (d) and (f) to ensure timely, efficient, and effective processing of reviews and to protect classified information from inadvertent disclosure. All referrals contained within accessioned records will be processed through the NDC.

a. Description. The referral process involves identification of information in records containing classified information that originated with another DoD Component or Executive Branch agency or the disclosure of which would affect the interests or activities of another DoD Component or Executive Branch agency and that could reasonably be expected to fall within one or more of the exemptions listed in subparagraph 13.b.(1) of this enclosure. Such records are eligible for referral. The referral process also requires formal notification of referral, making the records available for review, and recording final determinations.

b. Referral Responsibility. Identification of records eligible for referral is the responsibility of the primary reviewing agency and shall be completed prior to the date for automatic declassification established in accordance with section 12 of this enclosure. DoD Components shall use SF 715 to identify any record requiring referral.

16. MANDATORY DECLASSIFICATION REVIEW. Any individual or organization may request a declassification review of information classified pursuant to Reference (d) or previous classified national security information orders. Heads of the DoD Components shall establish processes for responding to such requests in accordance with Reference (f).

a. Information reviewed shall be declassified if it no longer meets the standards for classification established by this Volume. The declassified information shall be released unless withholding is authorized under other applicable law and the requirement of paragraph 1.e. of this enclosure.

b. Upon receiving a request for a mandatory declassification review, the responsible DoD organization shall conduct the review if:

(1) The request describes the document or material with enough specificity to allow DoD Component personnel to locate the records with a reasonable amount of effort. Requests for broad types of information, entire file series of records, or similar non-specific requests may be denied.

(2) The information falls under its purview.

(a) If documents or material being reviewed for declassification contain information originally classified by another DoD Component or U.S. Government agency or the disclosure of which would affect the interests or activities of another DoD Component or U.S. Government agency, the reviewing activity shall refer the appropriate portions of the request to the originating or affected organization. Unless the association of that organization with the requested information is itself classified, the DoD Component that received the review request shall notify the requester of the referral. The DoD Component that received the review request remains responsible for collecting all determinations made by organizations to which the information was referred and for informing the requestor of the final decision regarding declassification, unless other prior arrangements have been made.

(b) Requests for cryptologic information shall be processed in accordance with section 7 of this enclosure.

(c) The DoD Component that initially received or classified FGI shall determine whether the information is subject to a treaty or international agreement that does not permit unilateral declassification. (Refer also to section 20 of this enclosure.)

(3) The information is not the subject of pending litigation.

(4) The information is not contained within an operational file that is exempt from search and review, or disclosure, pursuant to sections 3141, 3142, 3143 and 3144 of Reference (af) or other applicable statute.

(5) The information has not been reviewed for declassification within the preceding 2 years. If the requested information has been reviewed for declassification within the 2 years preceding the request, the DoD Component shall notify the requester of the prior review decision and provide appeal rights information. No further review is required.

(6) The information was not originated by the incumbent President or the incumbent Vice President, the incumbent President's White House staff, or the incumbent Vice President's staff, committees, commissions, or boards appointed by the incumbent President, or other entities within the Executive Office of the President that solely advise and assist the incumbent President. Information so originated is exempt from the provisions of this section.

(7) The request was submitted to a Defense Intelligence Component by a U.S. citizen or an alien lawfully admitted for permanent residence; otherwise, the request may be denied.

c. A DoD Component may refuse to confirm or deny the existence or nonexistence of requested information when the fact of its existence or nonexistence is properly classified.

d. DoD Components shall either make a prompt declassification determination and notify the requester accordingly, or inform the requester of the additional time needed to process the request. DoD Components shall ordinarily make a final determination within 1 year from the date of receipt.

(1) In making a declassification determination DoD Components shall determine whether the information continues to meet the requirements for classification. Information to be withheld must not only qualify for classification under the criteria identified in paragraph 1.b of Enclosure 4, but there also must be a current basis for continued classification.

(2) When information cannot be declassified in its entirety, DoD Components shall make reasonable efforts to release, consistent with other applicable law and the requirements of paragraph 1.e. of this enclosure, those declassified portions of the requested information that constitute a coherent segment. Where information is withheld the specific reason, as specified by section 1.4 of Reference (d) and identified in paragraph 1.b of Enclosure 4 of this Volume, must be included for each redaction. Information that is redacted due to a statutory authority must be clearly marked with the specific authority that authorizes the redaction.

e. The mandatory declassification review process shall provide for administrative appeal in cases where the review results in the information remaining classified. The requester shall be notified of the results of the review and of the right to appeal, within 60 days of receipt, the denial of declassification. If the requester files an appeal, the DoD Component appellate authority shall make a determination within 60 working days following receipt. If additional time is required to make a determination, the appellate authority shall notify the requestor of the additional time needed and provide the reason for the extension. If the appeal is denied, the requester shall be notified of the right to appeal the denial to the ISCAP.

f. Requesters may be charged fees for processing their requests in accordance with the schedule of fees in Volume 11 A of DoD 7000.14-R (Reference (bj)).

17. SYSTEMATIC REVIEW FOR DECLASSIFICATION. Heads of the DoD Components that have classified information in accordance with Reference (d) or previous Executive orders shall establish systematic review programs to review for declassification information in the custody of the DoD Component. These programs shall review for declassification information that is contained in permanently valuable historical records that have been exempted from automatic declassification and shall determine if the information may be further exempt from automatic declassification in accordance with the provisions of this enclosure. These efforts shall be prioritized in accordance with the priorities established by the NDC.

18. DOWNGRADING CLASSIFIED INFORMATION. Downgrading information to a lower level of classification is appropriate when the information no longer requires protection at the originally assigned level and can be properly protected at a lower level. The principal purpose of downgrading is to conserve security resources by avoiding protection of information at too high a level. Any official with jurisdiction over the information who is authorized to classify or declassify the information may downgrade it.

a. Downgrading shall be considered when OCAs are deciding on the duration of classification to be assigned. If downgrading dates or events can be identified, they shall be specified along with the declassification instruction. Downgrading instructions do not replace declassification instructions.

b. An authorized official making a downgrading decision shall notify all known holders of the change in classification. If the information is subject to the Scientific and Technical Information Program (STIP) (DoDD 3200.12 (Reference (bk)), the authorized official shall also notify the Defense Technical Information Center.

c. When information is marked for downgrading on a specific date or event and that date or event has passed, holders shall confirm that the OCA(s) of the information has not extended the higher classification period prior to downgrading DoD information.

d. Downgraded information shall be marked as required by Enclosure 3 of Volume 2 of this Manual.

e. If a holder of classified information has reason to believe it should not be downgraded as indicated, the originator shall be notified through appropriate administrative channels. The document or material shall continue to be protected at the originally assigned classification until the issue is resolved.

19. UPGRADING CLASSIFIED INFORMATION. Classified information may be upgraded to a higher level of classification only by officials who have been delegated the appropriate level of OCA in accordance with Enclosure 4 of this Volume. The information to be upgraded must continue to meet the standards for classification specified in Enclosure 4 of this Volume. When making the decision to upgrade the classification level, OCAs shall consider the benefits to national security that will accrue from the higher classification against the costs associated with upgrading (e.g., the requirement for upgraded clearances or storage facilities, notification costs) and the ability to notify all holders of the information of the change so that the information shall be uniformly protected at the higher level. The OCA making the upgrading decision is responsible for notifying holders of the change in classification. For information subject to the STIP (Reference (bk)), the OCA shall also notify the Defense Technical Information Center. Upgraded information shall be marked as required by Enclosure 3 of Volume 2 of this Manual.

20. DECLASSIFYING FGI. Pursuant to Reference (d), FGI qualifies as an exemption to the automatic declassification rule. Within the Department of Defense, every effort shall be made to ensure that FGI is not subject to downgrading or declassification without the prior consent of the originating government. FGI may exist in two forms: foreign documents in possession of the Department of Defense, and foreign government classified information included within U.S. Government documents.

a. If FGI in the form of foreign documents in the possession of the Department of Defense constitute permanently valuable records of the U.S. Government and are subject to the 25-year automatic declassification rule, declassification officials shall consult with the originating foreign government to determine whether it consents to declassification. If the originating foreign government does not consent, the records shall be processed for exemption from automatic declassification in accordance with section 13 of this enclosure. The agency head shall determine whether exemption category 25X6, 25X9, or both should be applied.

b. U.S. Government documents that include classified FGI shall be marked with declassification instructions as specified in this enclosure and Volume 2 of this Manual. If these documents are permanently valuable records of the U.S. Government and are subject to the 25- year automatic declassification rule, the provisions of paragraph 20.a. of this section shall apply. A U.S. document marked as described herein cannot be downgraded below the highest level of FGI contained in the document or be declassified without the written permission of the foreign government or international organization that originated the information. Submit recommendations concerning downgrading or declassification to the DoD organization that created the document. If that organization supports the recommendation, it shall consult with the originating foreign government to determine whether that government consents to declassification.

c. DoD officials may consult directly with foreign governments regarding downgrading or declassification of FGI or seek assistance from the Department of State. In either case, DoD officials should first consult with the Director, International Security Programs, Defense Technology Security Administration, OUSD(P), for assistance and guidance.

21. APPLICATION OF DECLASSIFICATION AND EXTENSION OF CLASSIFICATION TO PRESENT AND PREDECESSOR EXECUTIVE ORDERS. The requirements for declassifying and extending classification specified by this enclosure apply to information classified in accordance with E.O. 12958 (Reference (bl)) and earlier Executive orders, as well as to information classified pursuant to Reference (d).

GLOSSARY

PART I. ABBREVIATIONS AND ACRONYMS

ACCM	alternative compensatory control measures
AO	agency official
B&P	bid and proposal
CI	Counterintelligence
CNWDI	Critical Nuclear Weapon Design Information
COMSEC	communication security
CUI	controlled unclassified information
CUIO	Controlled Unclassified Information Office
CUSR	Central U.S Registry
DAA	designated approval authority
DASD(NM)	Deputy Assistant Secretary of Defense for Nuclear Matters
DD	DoD
DIA	Defense Intelligence Agency
DNI	Director of National Intelligence
DoDD	DoD Directive
DoD CIO	DoD Chief Information Officer
DoDI	DoD Instruction
DoDM	DoD Manual
DSS	Defense Security Service
DUSD(I&S)	Deputy Under Secretary of Defense for Intelligence and Security
E.O.	Executive order
FGI	foreign government information
FOIA	Freedom of Information Act
FOUO	For Official Use Only
FRD	Formerly Restricted Data
GS	General Schedule
IA	information assurance
IAM	information assurance manager
IR&D	independent research and development
ISCAP	Interagency Security Classification Appeals Panel
ISOO	Information Security Oversight Office
ISSM	information system security officer
IT	information technology

MR	manual review
NARA	National Archives and Records Administration
NATO	North Atlantic Treaty Organization
NC2-ESI	Nuclear Command and Control-Extremely Sensitive Information
NDC	National Declassification Center
NSA	National Security Agency
NSA/CSS	National Security Agency/Central Security Service
NSC	National Security Council
OADR	originating agency's determination required
OCA	original classification authority
OPSEC	operations security
OUSD(I&S)	Office of the Under Secretary of Defense for Intelligence and Security
OUSD(P)	Office of the Under Secretary of Defense for Policy
RD	Restricted Data
SAO	Senior Agency Official
SAP	Special Access Program
SCI	sensitive compartmented information
SCIF	sensitive compartmented information facility
SF	standard form
SIPRNET	Secret Internet Protocol Router Network
SSO	special security officer
STIP	Scientific and Technical Information Program
TSCA	Top Secret control assistant
TSCO	Top Secret control officer
UCMJ	Uniform Code of Military Justice
U.S.C.	United States Code
USD(I&S)	Under Secretary of Defense for Intelligence and Security
USD(P)	Under Secretary of Defense for Policy
USSAN	United States Security Authority for NATO
WHS	Washington Headquarters Services

PART II. DEFINITIONS

Unless otherwise noted, these terms and their definitions are for the purpose of this Volume.

access. The ability or opportunity to obtain knowledge of classified information.

accessioned records. Records of permanent historical value in the legal custody of NARA.

activity security manager. The individual specifically designated in writing and responsible for the activity's information security program, which ensures that classified information (except SCI which is the responsibility of the SSO appointed by the senior intelligence official) and CUI are properly handled during their entire life cycle. This includes ensuring information is appropriately identified, marked, stored, disseminated, disposed of, and accounted for, as well as providing guidance on the handling of security incidents to minimize adverse effects and ensure that appropriate corrective action is taken. The security manager may be assigned responsibilities in other security disciplines such as personnel and physical security, etc. The activity security manager implements the information security program guidance established by this Manual and the Component senior agency official.

agency. Any Executive agency as defined in section 105 of Reference (ay); any Military Department as defined in section 102 of Reference (bd); and any other entity within the Executive Branch that comes into the possession of classified information.

authorized person. A person who has a favorable determination of eligibility for access to classified information, has signed an SF 312 nondisclosure agreement, and has a need to know for the specific classified information in the performance of official duties.

automatic declassification. The declassification of information based solely upon:

The occurrence of a specific date or event as determined by the OCA; or

The expiration of a maximum time frame for duration of classification established pursuant to Reference (d).

classification. The act or process by which information is determined to be classified information.

classification guidance. Any instruction or source that prescribes the classification of specific information.

classification guide. A documentary form of classification guidance issued by an OCA that identifies, for a specific subject, the elements of information that must be classified and establishes the level and duration of classification for each such element.

classified national security information. Information that has been determined pursuant to Reference (d), or any predecessor order, to require protection against unauthorized disclosure and is marked to indicate its classified status when in documentary form.

classifier. An individual who makes a classification determination and applies a security classification to information or material. A classifier may be an OCA or a person who derivatively assigns a security classification based on a properly classified source or a classification guide.

collateral information. All national security information classified Confidential, Secret, or Top Secret under the provision of an Executive order for which special systems of compartmentation (such as SCI or SAP) are not formally required.

compilation. An aggregation of preexisting items of information.

compromise. An unauthorized disclosure of classified information.

COMSEC. The protection resulting from all measures designed to deny unauthorized persons information of value that might be derived from the possession and study of telecommunications and to ensure the authenticity of such communications. COMSEC includes cryptosecurity, emission security, transmission security, and physical security of COMSEC material and information.

confidential source. Any individual or organization that has provided, or that may reasonably be expected to provide, information to the United States on matters pertaining to the national security with the expectation that the information or relationship, or both, are to be held in confidence.

control. The authority of the agency that originates information, or its successor in function, to regulate access to the information.

CUI. Unclassified information requiring safeguarding or dissemination controls, pursuant to and consistent with applicable law, regulations, and Government-wide policies. Some CUI may also be export-controlled or protected by contract. Release or disclosure of CUI to foreign governments or international organizations must be in accordance with Reference (z) and other policy and procedures established by the USD(P). See Volume 4 of this Manual for further information regarding CUI.

date of original classification. The date a document is determined to be classified. For example, classification would begin from the date a document is created, not from the date of any security classification guide used to authorize classification of that document.

damage to the national security. Harm to the national defense or foreign relations of the United States from the unauthorized disclosure of information, taking into consideration such aspects of the information as the sensitivity, value, utility, and provenance of that information.

declassification. The authorized change in the status of information from classified information to unclassified information.

declassification authority

The official who authorized the original classification, if that official is still serving in the same position;

The originator's current successor in function, if that individual has OCA;

A supervisory official of either the originator or his or her successor in function, if the supervisory official has OCA; or

Officials delegated declassification authority in writing by the agency head or the senior agency official.

declassification guide. Written instructions issued by a declassification authority that describes the elements of information regarding a specific subject that may be declassified and the elements that must remain classified. May also be a guide providing classification and declassification instructions specifically for information that is 25 years old or older and of permanent historical value. A declassification guide is the most commonly used vehicle for obtaining ISCAP approval of 25-year exemptions from the automatic declassification provisions of Reference (d).

Defense Intelligence Components. All DoD organizations that perform national intelligence, Defense Intelligence, and intelligence-related functions, including: the Defense Intelligence Agency; the National Geospatial-Intelligence Agency, the National Reconnaissance Office, the National Security Agency/Central Security Service, and the intelligence elements of the Active and Reserve components of the Military Departments, including the United States Coast Guard when operating as a service in the Navy.

derivative classification. Incorporating, paraphrasing, restating, or generating in new form information that is already classified, and marking the newly developed material consistent with the classification markings that apply to the source information. Includes the classification of information based on classification guidance. The duplication or reproduction of existing classified information is not derivative classification.

distribution statement. A statement used on a technical document to denote the extent of its availability for secondary distribution, release, and disclosure without additional approvals or authorizations. A distribution statement is distinct from and in addition to a security classification marking and any dissemination control markings included in the banner line. A distribution statement is also required on security classification guides submitted to the Defense Technical Information Center.

document. Any recorded information, regardless of the nature of the medium or the method or circumstances of recording. This includes any physical medium in or on which information is recorded or stored, to include written or printed matter, audiovisual materials, and electromagnetic storage media.

downgrading. A determination by a declassification authority that information classified and safeguarded at a specified level shall be classified and safeguarded at a lower level.

element of the Intelligence Community. See Intelligence Community.

equity. For purposes of classification management, information originally classified by or under the control of an agency.

exception. An approved permanent exclusion or deviation from an information security standard or requirement, as specified in this Volume.

exempted. Nomenclature and marking indicating information has been determined to fall within an enumerated exemption from automatic declassification in accordance with Reference (d).

FGI

Information provided to the U.S. Government by a foreign government or governments, an international organization of governments, or any element thereof, with the expectation that the information, the source of the information, or both, are to be held in confidence.

Information produced by the U.S. Government pursuant to or as a result of a joint arrangement with a foreign government or governments, or an international organization of governments, or any element thereof, requiring that the information, the arrangement, or both, are to be held in confidence.

Information received and treated as FGI pursuant to the terms of a predecessor order to Reference (d).

file series. File units or documents arranged according to a filing system or kept together because they relate to a particular subject or function, result from the same activity, document a specific kind of transaction, take a particular form, or have some other relationship arising out of their creation, receipt, or use, such as restrictions on access or use. Also documentary material, regardless of its physical form or characteristics, that is arranged in accordance with a filing system or maintained as a unit because it pertains to the same subject, function, or activity.

file series exemption. An exception to the 25-year automatic declassification provisions of Reference (d). This exception applies to entire blocks of records, i.e., "file series," within an agency's records management program. To qualify for this exemption, the file series must be replete with exemptible information.

FOUO. A protective marking to be applied to unclassified information when disclosure to the public of that particular record, or portion thereof, would reasonably be expected to cause a foreseeable harm to an interest protected by one or more provisions of the FOIA. This includes information that qualifies for protection pursuant to the provisions of the Privacy Act of 1974, as amended. See Reference (bk) for detailed information on categories of information that may qualify for exemption from public disclosure. The use of FOUO marking remains in effect until the revised Volume 4 of this Manual is released.

FRD. Information removed from the RD category upon a joint determination by the Department of Energy (or antecedent agencies) and the Department of Defense that such information relates primarily to the military utilization of atomic weapons and that such information can be safeguarded adequately as classified defense information. For purposes of foreign dissemination, this information is treated in the same manner as RD.

heads of DoD activities. Heads, either military or civilian, of organizations, commands, and staff elements subordinate to a DoD Component, with jurisdiction over and responsibility for the execution of the organization's mission and functions, including its information security program. The official may carry the title of commander, commanding officer, or director, or other equivalent title.

human intelligence source. People who provide intelligence directly; individuals associated with organizations (such as foreign government entities and intelligence services) who willingly share intelligence information with the United States; individuals and organizations who facilitate the placement or service of technical collection means that could not succeed without their support; and foreign citizens who are identified as of an intelligence interest to the United States with a reasonable expectation that they will provide information or services in the future. Information that may reveal the identities of people upon whom the United States relies for information, access to information, or cooperation leading to obtaining information is considered to potentially reveal human intelligence sources.

information. Any knowledge that can be communicated or documentary material, regardless of its physical form or characteristics, that is owned by, produced by or for, or is under the control of the U.S. Government.

information security. The system of policies, procedures, and requirements established in accordance with Reference (d) to protect information that, if subjected to unauthorized disclosure, could reasonably be expected to cause damage to national security. The term also applies to policies, procedures, and requirements established to protect unclassified information that may be withheld from release to the public pursuant to Executive order, statute, or regulation.

integral file block. A distinct component of a file series that should be maintained as a separate unit to ensure the integrity of the records. An integral file block may consist of a set of records covering either a specific topic or a range of time, such as a Presidential administration or a 5-year retirement schedule within a specific file series that is retired from active use as a group. For purposes of automatic declassification, integral file blocks shall contain only records dated within 10 years of the oldest record in the file block.

integrity. The state that exists when information is unchanged from its source and has not been accidentally or intentionally modified, altered, or destroyed.

Intelligence Community. An element or agency of the U.S. Government identified in or designated pursuant to section 3(4) of the National Security Act of 1947, as amended, or section 3.5(h) of Reference (ah).

international program. Any program, project, contract, operation, exercise, training, experiment, or other initiative that involves a DoD Component or a DoD contractor and a foreign government, international organization, or corporation that is located and incorporated to do business in a foreign country.

material. Any product or substance on or in which information is embodied.

national security. The national defense or foreign relations of the United States. National security includes defense against transnational terrorism.

national security system. Defined in section 3542(b)(2) of Reference (av).

need to know. A determination that a prospective recipient requires access to specific classified information in order to perform or assist in a lawful and authorized governmental function.

network. A system of two or more computers that can exchange data or information.

newly discovered records. Records that were inadvertently not reviewed prior to the effective date of automatic declassification because the Agency declassification authority was unaware of their existence.

OCA. An individual authorized in writing, either by the President, the Vice President, or by agency heads or other officials designated by the President, to originally classify information (i.e., to classify information in the first instance).

original classification. An initial determination that information requires, in the interests of national security, protection against unauthorized disclosure.

pass/fail. A declassification technique that regards information at the full document level. Any exemptible portion of a document may result in exemption (failure) of the entire document. Documents that contain no exemptible information are passed and therefore declassified. Documents that contain exemptible information are failed and therefore exempt from automatic declassification.

permanent records. Any Federal record that has been determined by NARA to have sufficient value to warrant its preservation in the National Archives of the United States. Permanent records include all records accessioned by NARA into the National Archives of the United States and later increments of the same records, and those for which the disposition is permanent on SF 115, "Request for Records Disposition Authority," approved by NARA on or after May 14, 1973.

permanently valuable records. See "records having permanent historical value."

RD. All data concerning design, manufacture, or utilization of atomic weapons; the production of special nuclear material; or the use of special nuclear material in the production of energy, but not data declassified or removed from the RD category pursuant to section 2162 of The Atomic Energy Act of 1954, as amended.

records. The records of an agency and Presidential papers or Presidential records, as those terms are defined in Reference (av), including those created or maintained by a U.S. Government contractor, licensee, certificate holder, or grantee that are subject to the sponsoring agency's control in accordance with the terms of the contract, license, certificate, or grant.

records having permanent historical value. Records that the Archivist of the United States has determined should be maintained permanently in accordance with Reference (av).

records management. The planning, controlling, directing, organizing, training, promoting, and other managerial activities involved with respect to records creation, records maintenance and use, and records disposition in order to achieve adequate and proper documentation of the policies and transactions of the Federal Government and effective and economical management of agency operations. Within the Department of Defense, records management is implemented by Reference (aw).

redaction. For purposes of declassification, the removal of exempted information from copies of a document.

released to the public. Made available to the general public through any publicly accessible media or method.

risk management. The process of identifying, assessing, and controlling risks and making decisions that balance risk with cost and benefits.

safeguarding. Measures and controls that are prescribed to protect classified information.

SAP. A program established for a specific class of classified information that imposes safeguarding and access requirements that exceed those normally required for information at the same classification level. In the Department of Defense, any DoD program or activity (as authorized in Reference (d)), employing enhanced security measures (e.g., safeguarding, access requirements), exceeding those normally required for collateral information at the same level of classification, shall be established, approved, and managed as a DoD SAP in accordance with Reference (q).

scheduled records. All records that fall under a NARA-approved records control schedule.

SCI. Classified information concerning or derived from intelligence sources, methods, or analytical processes that is required to be handled within formal access control systems established by the Director of National Intelligence.

security classification guide. A documentary form of classification guidance issued by an OCA that identifies the elements of information regarding a specific subject that must be classified and establishes the level and duration of classification for each such element.

security clearance. A determination that a person is eligible in accordance with the standards of Reference (s) for access to classified information.

self-inspection. The internal review and evaluation of individual DoD Component activities and the DoD Component as a whole with respect to the implementation of the information security program established in accordance with References (b), (d) and (f), and this Manual.

senior agency official. An official appointed by the head of a DoD Component to be responsible for direction, administration, and oversight of the Component's information security program, to include classification, declassification, safeguarding, and security education and training programs, and for the efficient and effective implementation of References (b), (d), (e), and (f) and the guidance in this Manual. Where used in reference to authorities pursuant to section 5.4(d) of Reference (d), this term applies only to the senior agency officials of the Military Departments and of the Department of Defense.

senior intelligence official. The highest ranking military or civilian charged with direct foreign intelligence missions, functions, or responsibilities with a department, agency, component, or element of an Intelligence Community organization. Responsible for direction, administration, and oversight of the organization's SCI program, to include classification, declassification, safeguarding, and security education and training programs for the effective implementation of References (b), (j), and (ad) and the guidance in this Manual.

SSO. Individual appointed, in accordance with References (j) and (ad), by the senior intelligence official to be responsible for the day-to-day security management, operation, implementation, use, and dissemination of SCI within an activity.

tab. A narrow paper sleeve placed around a document or group of documents in such a way that it is readily visible.

telecommunications. The preparation, transmission, or communication of information by electronic means.

transferred records. Records transferred to agency storage facilities or a Federal records center.

unauthorized disclosure. Communication or physical transfer of classified or controlled unclassified information to an unauthorized recipient.

unscheduled records. Records whose final disposition has not been approved by NARA.

U.S. entity

State, local, or tribal governments.

State, local, and tribal law enforcement and firefighting entities.

Public health and medical entities.

Regional, State, local, and tribal emergency management entities, including State Adjutants General and other appropriate public safety entities.

Private sector entities serving as part of the Nation's critical infrastructure and/or key resources.

violation

Any knowing, willful, or negligent action that could reasonably be expected to result in an unauthorized disclosure of classified information.

Any knowing, willful, or negligent action to classify or continue the classification of information contrary to the requirements of Reference (d), its implementing directives, or this Manual.

Any knowing, willful, or negligent action to create or continue a special access program contrary to the requirements of Reference (d), Reference (q), or this Manual.

waiver. An approved temporary or short-term exclusion or deviation from an information security standard or requirement, as specified in this Volume.

weapons of mass destruction. Any weapon of mass destruction as defined in section 1801(p) of Reference (af).

Notes:

Notes:

Notes:

Notes:

Notes:

Notes:

Notes:

Notes:

Notes:

Notes:

Notes:

Notes:

Notes:

Notes:

Notes:

Notes:

Books

This book, other security and NISP books and training are also available at our website. Helpful books include those part of the *Security Clearances and Cleared Defense Contractor* series by Red Bike Publishing:

- Insider's Guide to Security Clearances
- How to Get U.S. Government Contracts and Classified Work
- National Industrial Security Program Operating Manual (NISPOM)
- Self Inspection Guidebook for NISP Contractors
- International Traffic In Arms Regulation (ITAR)

Training
Training topics include the following at https://www.nispomcentral.com:

- SF-312 Non Disclosure Briefing
- Insider Threat Training
- Derivative Classifier Training
- Security Awareness Training

Also at NISPOM Central (www.nispomcentral.com)
NISPOM Fundamentals Course-Training that discusses each chapter of the NISPOM in depth; more than 8 hours of recorded training

- Alternatively, you can take course one chapter or topic at a time
- Great study material. Each course provides completion certificates that can be used to earn CEUs for recertification.

Made in the USA
Monee, IL
05 November 2026

67911923R00059